Uncover Software Specifications Using High-Level Design

Discover Hidden Requirements and Constraints to Improve Quality and Reduce Rework

Uncover Software Specifications Using High-Level Design: Discover Hidden Requirements and Constraints to Improve Quality and Reduce Rework

First Edition. (2023)

Table of Contents

Table of Figures

Table of Tables

Preface

After working as a consultant for 19-plus years now—meeting customers daily, attending workshops, and listening to business issues to develop solutions—I wondered why IT transformation often fails to deliver the expected results. It took me a few years to gather enough knowledge across multiple fields to build a big picture. During the journey, I discovered, much to my surprise, that information technology organizations fail in the basics, or even neglect some components, leading to a deficit in the digital transformation. This was when I started drafting the IT transformation guide for the next-generation IT (IT-TNG framework).

The *IT-TNG framework* is focused on practitioners, not on theoretical knowledge. Each guide helps a practitioner achieve a specific function using tested methods and concepts from the industry. I also wanted to empower the readers in their careers by including a bit of business in the books. This is relevant because when a subject matter expert like a developer, business analyst (BA), or administrator understands topics like strategy, decision-making, and value, their management typically notices, which is often advantageous in their careers.

Each book balances theories, practical steps, and management practices. This structure aims to empower whoever reads these books in their current role and provide them with the knowledge to take a more prominent role in the organization.

The IT-TNG framework consists of the following practices:

- Process: Process reengineering
- Digital solution: How to develop a digital solution
- Solution HL design: Align requirements to design
- Services: How to build a service offering to the customer
- Value support: How to support a service in the best possible manner
- Value maintenance: How to control the technical aspects of a service

- Service adjustments: Decision-making and service components adjustment
- Value realization: Promote and discover services
- Innovation: Generate innovative ideas to solve business challenges
- Strategy and effort orchestration: Developing synergies from all practices

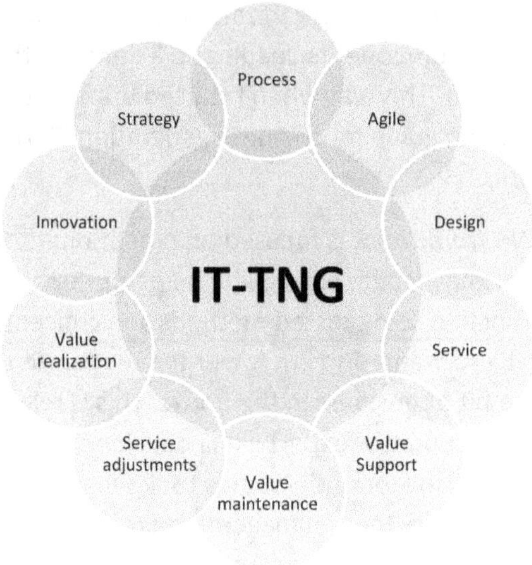

Figure 1 IT-TNG framework

Each of these modules is independent, and although each represents a layer in IT that should not be neglected when considering digital transformation, two or more practices generate synergy and start driving improvement. A single practice will drive value, but you need at least three practices to drive the digital transformation forward.

The organization might already have a functioning practice representing one aspect of the IT-TNG. In such a case, keep it as is. The idea is to build the missing parts of the 10 core practices regardless of efficiency. And once you create the whole stack, you can go back to optimize these practices.

While writing the IT-TNG, I followed a focused approach with two principles in mind:

- 80/20 rule
- Law of diminishing returns

The 80/20 rule means you don't need many initiatives to achieve the best results. You only need a handful of initiatives to reach a strategic position. The law of diminishing returns means that with every improvement, you gain less, so it's about finding the pressure point and pressing to get the maximum results with the least effort. I also considered the unintended effects of applying these practices. For example, thinking critically about a software design unintendedly challenges the value, reduces change requests, and increases business alignment.

This is what all of these practice guides are about, the minimum possible resource investments that will drive value.

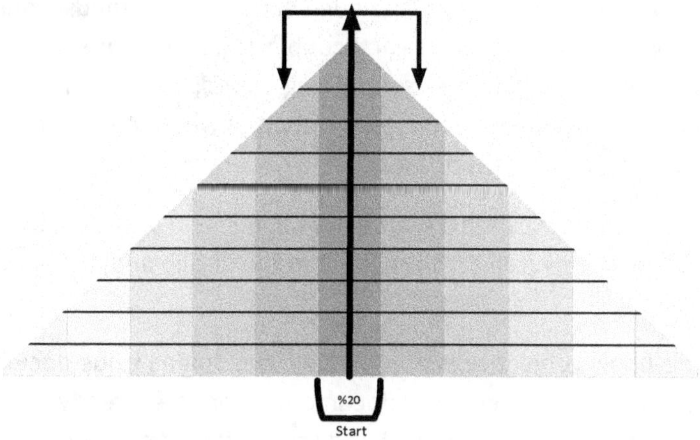

Figure 2 Ten practices stack

The practices have no specific order, but there are 10 levels. Start with the core activities in each layer, and once all ten practices are stacked, you begin expanding each practice layer based on the organization's need. If you try to grow one layer before making the core stack of all 10 layers, you will hit the collective ceiling blocking value realization, regardless of investment. To avoid hitting this and wasting resources, you should build the initial layers first to proceed in a value-adding manner.

How to Get in Touch with Me

You might have a question or need clarification to adapt the ideas discussed in this book to your situation. Please feel free to drop me an email at Ahmed.Hussein@ITTNG.com.

The Expected Audience for This Book

This book is for business analysts and software engineers (programmers). It does not require any programming knowledge, nor does it require prior experience in design or databases.

In this book, business analysts expand their toolkit to obtain more precise requirements by mapping them to design, application models, and databases; following this model helps in articulating the problem and eliciting the requirements from a group that cannot directly provide exact requirements. Each chapter in this book covers a single topic. Though each chapter stands alone, some areas are still related. The first couple of chapters provide a quick overview of requirements-gathering tactics. Also, the final chapter includes a summary and consideration of when the application goes into the deployment phase.

Another benefit of this book is that it will help provide a clear path and reduce overall technical debt in the design and architecture phases.

This book's objective is to produce a customer's value document and not a purely technical document. There are already plenty of good books and materials that discuss detailed code or software architecture. So, the focus will be on validating customer value from the customer perspective, not the development side.

Book Road Map and How It's Mapped to Application Parts

To produce a successful application that is aligned with the customer's requirements, you must collect all the application parts, though some will not be visible to the end user/customer. But you need to understand them properly to build the application correctly and allow enough flexibility for future changes.

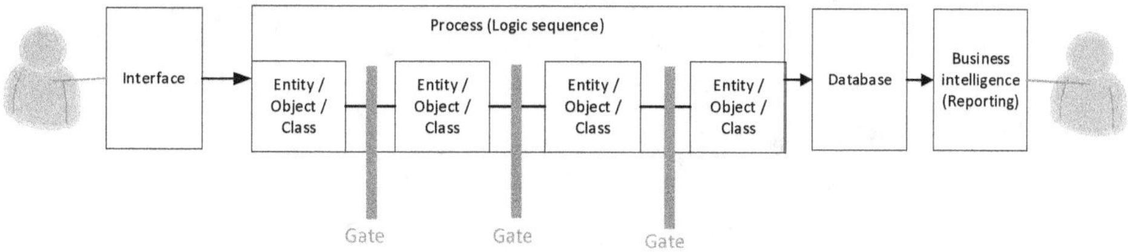

Figure 3 *Application composition*

A traditional application is a composition of:

- Interface (screens to enter or display data)
- Objects/entities or classes
- A method/activity or action (the problem it will solve)
- A gate to validate the application actions (business rules)
- The overall process flow
- The databases (to store the data)
- The reporting (the data generated and arranged in a particular way to be helpful for the end user)

Most of the changes will be in the parts the users interact with for convenience or functionality. The interface will keep changing, and the report requirements will change. Sometimes, you will need to capture additional information in the interface to generate the report properly. To gather these requirements, several iterations may be necessary in order to decide what to do.

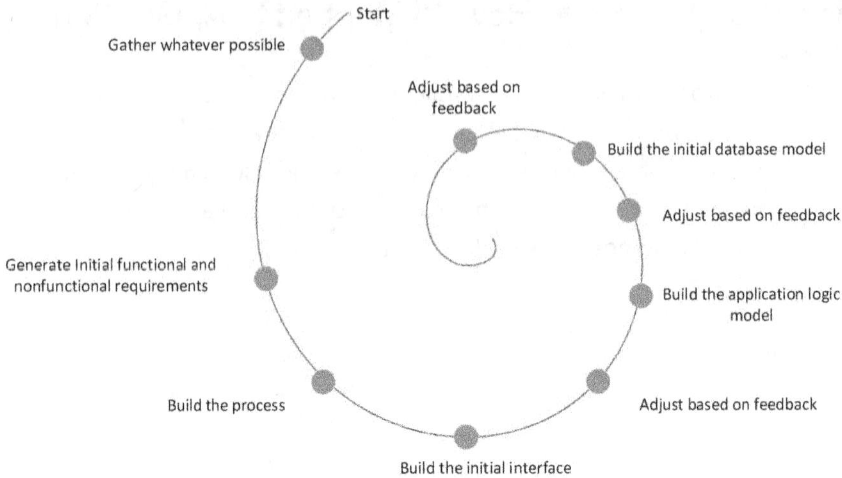

Figure 4 Requirements changes

The starting point is to gather whatever you can from the stakeholders, though this is not the book's focus.

This book's suggested process should be finished within two weeks (design sprint). Though it seems more of a Waterfall approach, following this suggested schedule is the most efficient way of jump-starting the project:

Day 1: Kick off the project. Meet with the project manager, sponsor, and project team. Define your stakeholders.

Day 2: Gather knowledge about the project plan. Schedule the meetings, prepare for the interviews, and plan the workshops for the next two days.

Day 3: Conduct workshops to gather information.

Day 4: Hold interviews to gather information.

Day 5: Present the findings in a meeting. Plan the next meeting.

Day 6: Plan and draw the interface frames/screens with the stakeholders and the subject matter expert (SME). Plan and design the reports needed with the SME.

Day 7: Consolidate the screens and present the final views.

Day 8: Plan the database requirements with the SME.

Day 9: Draw the application models with the SME.

Day 10: Consolidate and present the findings to the stakeholder group.

The major risk to this schedule is the stakeholders' availability, so this needs to be planned to ensure the schedule should be as compact as possible.

Chapter 1: Gather the Initial Requirements

Let's start with a simple exercise: Close your eyes and think of a car. Next, ask a few people to do the same. Most likely, you will not get the same answer from everyone. This is why getting a group of people to agree on look, function, and performance is difficult—everyone builds their expectations based on their background and history. Additionally, some users/customers/stakeholders cannot articulate their needs properly, or make nearly impossible requests (technology limitations). So, the first step is to gather whatever is possible using traditional means.

Collecting Requirements

This is the initial phase of understanding the project scope for the project manager and the project sponsor.

Tip: During a conversation with stakeholders, watch out for areas out of scope for the project. Sometimes, a stakeholder will not be able to make a decision. In this case, offer alternatives from which they can select one.

Requirement Gathering

Requirement gathering happens in several ways. Most notable are:

- Interviews.
- Brainstorming sessions, focus group.
- Observing a job or a process.
- Surveying.
- Requirements gathering workshop. Cocreating a big picture during the workshop ensures a shared understanding of the solution's vision, why to build it, goals and objectives, and the high-level scope.

The worst situation is when someone discovers missing requirements in the middle of the project; sometimes, they can be added and other times reworked, but project modification is required. Correct business requirement analysis will save much rework, and there are steps to follow to identify the requirements as accurately as possible. It is the discovery process; analyze, summarize, and document the requirements before moving to the next steps.

Identify Stakeholders

A stakeholder is a crucial person in the project. They have something to gain or lose from the project, are impacted by the work, or influence the project; it is essential to know their requirements and interests. In some cases, all the users are stakeholders, but since it is impossible to list and to interview all users, we use a sample to represent the entire user group. The first step to identifying stakeholders is to sit down and brainstorm with the sponsor and project manager as to who might be involved. They may be people or other organizations as well. Mention them all by person/department/organization name. Avoid generic terms.

Internal	**External**
Boss	The main vendor (Jim Q. Vendor)
VP	The supplier (John M. Supplier)
Users	
The technical support team	
Finance department (John Doe)	

Table 1 *Stakeholder examples*

The entire project team should create this list, not a single person. Always ensure that the majority of the stakeholders know the exact outcome of the project to avoid any potential negative impact. Sometimes, you will need to fish for the stakeholders (the hidden ones). Sometimes, you might do a mass emailing with a Zoom/team/Webex call and meeting agenda explaining the project with the project manager. This is not the project kickoff. This is a casual call to explain the problem and the desired outcome. Anyone attending should be included as a potential stakeholder.

Identify Business Requirements

In this step, collect from the identified stakeholders the requirements needed. Each of the stakeholders considers the project only from their perspective; they may identify requirements far beyond the project scope. In such a case, gather the requirement as it might be helpful later on, but note it as "considered for the next project." Expectation management is critical in this stage.

Requirements *eliciting* is asking a question (the right question). The requirements *analysis* is understanding the answers and discovering new questions leading to how the pieces connect.

Collection Techniques

There are two main techniques:

An interview, where you will talk to each one of the stakeholders. A guided interview is preferable. Create simple questions in advance to guide the interview properly.

Focus groups and workshops will provide input while showing the integration points between departments.

You typically start with focus groups to build the requirements skeleton, and later you do one-on-one interviews to get more details. Usually, two or three sessions with groups will identify 60% of the requirements. Three individual one-on-one meetings will add 10% to 25% additional details. The remaining 15% to 30% could be discovered using these methods, but the duration it takes to find it is quite long, so usually it's discovered during the project.

Categorize Features

It is required to categorize features as to:

- The importance of the feature (time/budget limitations)
- The type of feature (what is core for the minimum viable product to go live)

The Importance of the Features

After the core information is collected from the stakeholders, the last question should be "Why do they need such a feature?" Is it a "must," "should," or "nice to have" feature? Always ask stakeholders to categorize requirements into the following groups:

- **Must** feature is the core feature that the business depends on.
- **Should** feature is a core feature that will speed the cycle of the software (like simple reporting functionality).
- **Nice to have** is a feature designed for user comfort and ease of access.

In case the stakeholder does not know how to prioritize the requirements, use MoSCoW prioritization: gather every requirement available and assume we will not deliver any of them. The impact of not doing a requirement will determine whether it is a must have, should have, could have, or nice to have.

Note: When users mark every feature as a must have, or when in doubt, force the normal distribution. In other words, the users may select from the total list only 15% as must, 70% as should, and 15% as nice to have.

Categorize the Types

Once all the requirements are collected from all stakeholders, begin categorizing them into the following groups:

- **Functional**: This is what the solution should do (for example, responding to orders in less than five seconds).
- **Nonfunctional**: The situation and environment the solution operates in (for example, the uptime for a solution must be 99.99% of the time).
- **Technical requirements**: These requirements are related to how the system is built, like the OS type and server configuration.
- **Transition requirement** (temporary): For example, if an old system served a specific function and migrated its old data into the new system.

Requirements Refinement and Verification

Ensure that the collected requirements reflect the current business strategies. To identify these, you will need to work with the solution's subject matter experts (SMEs):

- What requirements should be dropped
- The simplicity of building this requirement (ranking)

- The grouping of the requirements (patch 1, patch 2, etc.)

This information will be needed to plan the sprints and the release schedule (timeline). And finally, conduct a workshop to verify all gathered requirements and their groups. Address the requirements that have been dropped and why.

There are some exercises to perform before you start getting into the actual software drawing. If you don't conduct this part correctly, you are missing many requirements and taking a considerable risk, even if you are Agile or do continuous delivery. You need to understand the *why* before a single line of code is written.

The three tools to use to validate your understanding are:

Fishbone diagram: This simple diagram will allow you to drill down to discover the issue the system is trying to solve.

Mind map: This is to ensure you understand everything in a well-connected manner, and you will challenge the stereotypical thinking or the implicit requirements.

Flowchart and swimlane: It's all about value, and without understanding how things move from one actor to the next, you will not discover the real function the new system is trying to fulfill. Drawing a flowchart first is important to confirm the general understanding of the process.

Define a Bigger Problem

Small, additional issues and system limitations will surface through interviews with users. This may be a symptom of a broader issue. For this, use a fishbone diagram. It's a fast and straightforward QA and problem analysis tool. It's a good practice since you have already engaged with the stakeholders and have access to conduct workshops to draw and define the main problem.

First, draw a line to represent the main problem. Start branching out, adding "bones" to represent issues that result from the primary problem.

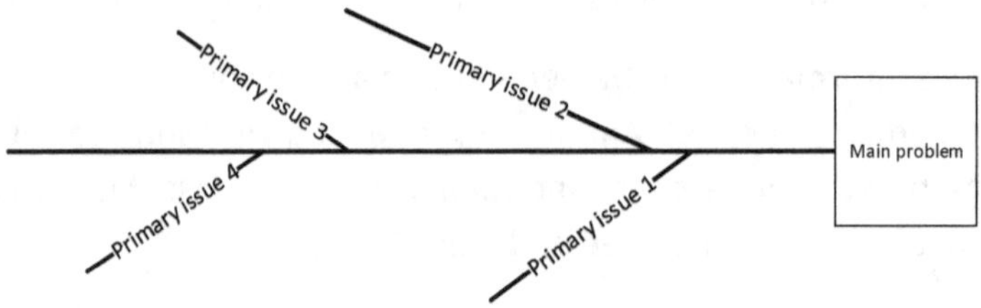

Figure 5 Main problem

This step, though simple, will confirm that all the sub-issues come from one main problem. Avoid a situation where there is no direct relationship between the requirements gathered and the main problem. This could be a complicated project to close and a highly complex design if this is the case.

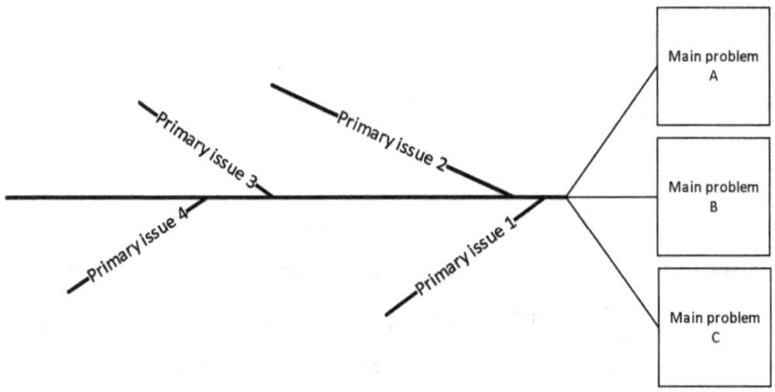

Figure 6 Multiple problems

If this is the situation, separate the problems into different fishbones and create a project road map for solving each. It could be one software program with multiple modules *or* multiple independent systems. As mentioned, one system needs to solve *one* problem. The more problems the system solves, the more difficult it may be to change or update. Multiple systems could hide behind one interface, but the process and logic must be separate.

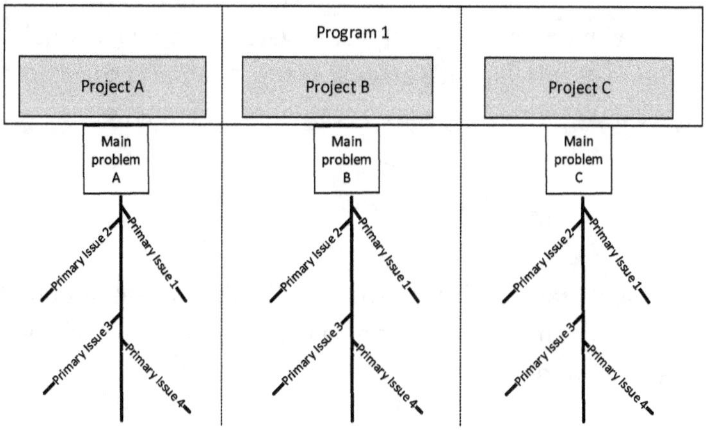

Figure 7 Multi-problem fix

The next step is to draw secondary issues branching from each primary issue. If possible, generate at least two or three from each primary issue.

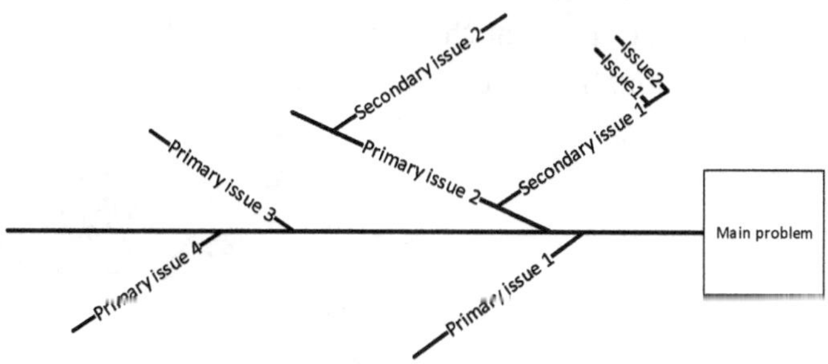

Figure 8 Fishbone diagram

Usually, the stakeholders don't have a causal relationship between the primary and secondary issues. So, start with each primary issue in different mediums to focus on only one issue at a time. For example, using a flip chart, break down one issue on each page. To validate all of that, move to mind maps to confirm the logic.

Mind Map, a Brainstorming Tool

Mind mapping is a thinking and brainstorming tool. There are many requirements, some of which are user interface–based, some performance-based, and some application functions, among many more possibilities. A mind map is used to ensure the correct understanding of things and to avoid logic gaps in the requirements. Start with the main topic (the software or a primary issue). In most mind map software, it's an oval shape, but you can just write the word if you wish. There is no restriction or limitation.

Now add branches. These are the thoughts you get around this application. It could be anything you think about when you think of the application.

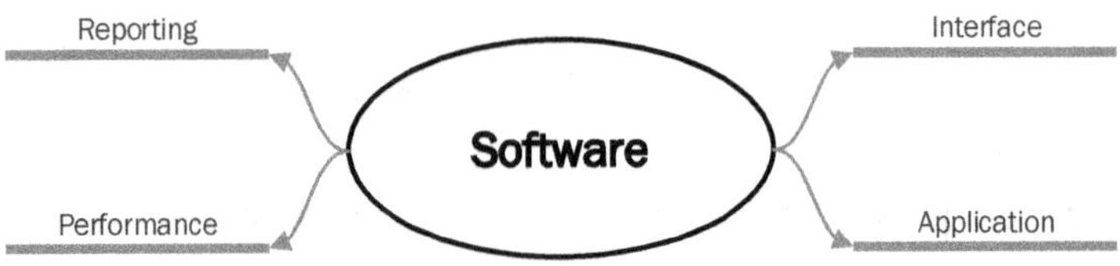

Now pick one of the branches you created in the previous step and write your thoughts about it, implicit and explicit.

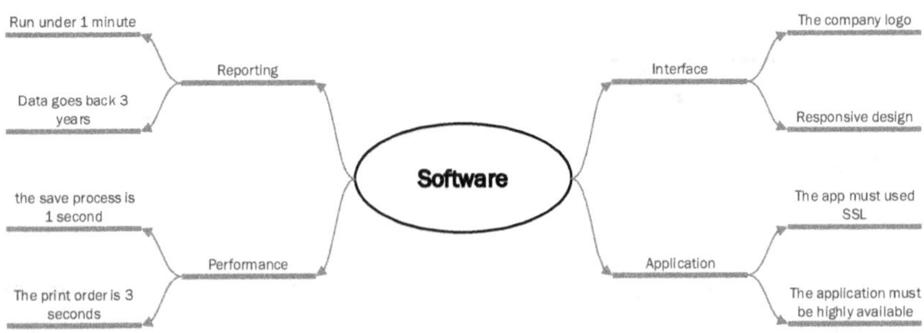

Figure 9 Mind map example

Ideas will start rolling out. Don't try to stop the flow. Just follow the logical process. Whatever you think is OK and makes sense, by all means, add it. Keep adding until no more ideas come to mind.

It's worth noting that this is not a standard process. This is free-form. You can change branches, move branches around, and adjust and rewire them as you see fit because the more you think about them, the more connections you discover.

Also, please note that this is an individual exercise. In other words, you are the only one who will see this, and, usually, you don't ask stakeholders and other team members about this.

Now go back to the stakeholder requirements and compare what you wrote to what they requested. Most likely, you will have two cases:

- Things you thought about but don't exist (logical to you, but no one talked about it for some reason)
- Items they requested, but you did not include

Start with the second case, add it to the diagram, and start brainstorming around it. If you can come up with additional topics or requirements, that would be very good.

Now for the requirements that don't map to the customer requirements that you defined: you need to go back to the stakeholders and challenge them on why they are not included. The idea is that the more you do this exercise, the more you reduce the chance of something being forgotten. Unlike other prototyping techniques, this exercise is simple enough and can be done in one hour or less.

Any business is a set of processes (systems) that deliver value to an end customer. Understanding the new system position in the value chain between the operations and the end customer is essential to providing the value required. Often (more than we like to admit), some systems are unnecessary and could be removed from the value delivery chain. Always consider the value as the target: "no value" equals "no system." This is why pointing out all the requirements to solve one main problem, as shown in the previous steps, is so important. If no relationship exists to solve the problem, the business driver for this system doesn't exist, which could be a bad indicator.

Business Process Modeling

The software you are trying to build has a process—even if only a small process inside a larger one. A process is a transformation action toward one or more goals. It's measurable, has a specific result, and has a specific trigger to start it. So, the next logical step after gathering the initial requirements is to document the process flow to understand where the application fits. You either have a greenfield environment (no previous process exists) or a process already in the current organization. Since the second option includes the first one, in the next part we will assume this is so. Documenting these processes is critical for an organization to stay competitive.

Business process modeling (BPM) is a visual way the organization keeps track of its processes. Moreover, it helpsto make sure the processes match its goals and objectives. The main benefit is understanding how the organization runs and performs activities and to help identify vague or missing processes.

The first step in BPM is to identify the steps included in the process. The business analyst (BA) uses diagramming tools to visually represent a process to ensure that everyone's understanding is the same andavoid issues in project delivery and development down the road.

Discover and Draw the Current Process

Before contemplating any improvement in existing processes, it is crucial to know the organization's current setup status. Any spontaneous move to enforce a process or develop a capability that conflicts with the existing business will result in project failure.

The idea behind all of these BPM diagrams is to have a reference point that will focus on what is needed. Typically, hundreds of processes in any given organization exist. Upgrading or modifying any components requires knowledge of the data used and the person who deals with it. Otherwise, you risk impacting other processes or creating a zombie process that takes up resources but does not generate any value. Therefore, before any change, a deeper and more informed understanding of the entity, its activities, and its data flow is required.

How to Document a Current System

The process of documenting the existing processes has three main steps:

1. Interview stakeholders and create an activity list
2. Build data flow diagrams
3. Build flowcharts and swimlanes

To make this happen quickly, plan the first half of the day as a 1:1 interview with the process owner; this takes one hour and an arranged two-hour session with a group of users who use the process daily to build the process branches. The remainder of the day is used to create the activity list, the process steps, and the flow diagrams. This setup allows getting back to the users for questions on the same day.

Create an Activities List

The first step is to build a responsibility matrix by going to the owner (if no owner is available, turn to the frequent users) and asking how the existing process and its variations function. This becomes a what-if scenario: Create a new table whenever a new branch starts for a new activity. Document the narrative and start building the activity table. Any activity requires an entity or an action to trigger it. Typically, this will be a request or an issue.

Let's take building a support request as an example. Sit down with a support representative to ask about the process of printers, for example. Here is what you might learn:

*In **IT support**, there are many cases related to **printers**. Sometimes, we need to start an order for a new printer. In other cases, it's just the driver installed on the system, or sometimes just a minor issue in the printer that can be easily fixed by the **user**, like a paper jam. In other cases, it requires IT or **toner** replacement or for the printer to be sent to the **manufacturer** for maintenance.*

*Boldface words are shown as entities in our activity list.

Start with IT's first scenario—to get a new printer for the user (this is the first branch). Get details on the process followed to make an acquisition. Get details for the steps involved.

The user contacts IT using a phone or email to request a printer. The request is sent to the user's manager via email for approval. Once approved, the approval is sent to the purchasing department for the printer acquisition. The supplier delivers the printer. IT engineers collect it from the warehouse and move it to the end-user location. Users will grant us access to work on their laptops. We install and make the necessary configurations. Once done, the user tests the printer and provides us with the sign-off.

*This overview represents the IT point of view.

From the detailed description above, we can now extract an activity list.

Entities	Activities
User	1. Contact IT support.
IT support/ helpdesk	2. Pick up the phone, read email. 3. Read/listen to the requests. **4. Write request approval for the user's manager.**
Manager	**5. Approve/Reject**
IT	6. Send the approval to the purchasing department. *or* Notify the user of rejection.
Purchasing	7. Send a request to the supplier.
Supplier	8. Deliver the printer.
Warehouse	9. Receive the printer. **10. Notify IT via email.**
IT support/ helpdesk	11. Collect the printer from the warehouse. **12. Update the record with supplier warranty.** 13. Deliver the printer to the user location.
User	**14. Grant access to the machine**
IT support/ helpdesk	15. Install the printer. **16. Make the necessary configurations.**
User	**17. Test the printer.** **18. Provide sign-off.**
IT support/ helpdesk	**19. File the sign-off.**

Table 2 Activity list example

Using the list in Table 2, describe the entities: Are they internal (controlled by IT) or external (IT cannot control)? Describe the activities: Do they involve data processing? (Do they change the state of information?) Or is data merely moved? Data processing is marked in bold in the table, and external entities are underlined. Use the data generated from the narrative (the activity list), and proceed with drawing diagrams:

- Context diagram
- Physical data flow diagram (PDFD)
- Logical data flow diagram (LDFD)

The primary shapes used in these diagrams are shown in Table 3.

Shape	Meaning
	External entity
	Internal entities/activities
	Datastore
	Data flow

Table 3 Diagram shapes

Context Diagram

This diagram provides a high-level, at-a-glance view of internal and external entities. The internal entity is the organization. The external entity can be a supplier or bank. Or it can be a department, team, system, or process within the organization that interacts with external entities. This might be characterized as an us-or-them diagram. The external entities are not the focus of the context diagram. The main reason for creating a context diagram is to understand the interaction between the primary entity (*the system* in our example) and the interactions and dependencies with other systems. Later on, it will point to other processes in the system that need further documentation because each arrow represents a process or subprocess.

Drawing a context diagram is relatively simple. Start by drawing the first context diagram with the system and external entities. Then, find its internal entity and draw a new context diagram in each external entity. Keep doing this until all relevant entities have context diagrams—these additional diagrams to better understand the dependency chain.

The context diagram is meant to define system boundaries. It is a logical, abstract diagram. To build a context diagram, follow three steps:

- **Step 1**: Start by writing the process name being documented. (This shape will link to all the internal entities.)
- **Step 2**: Write the names of all external entities, each one in a separate box.
- **Step 3**: Add arrows, each with an abstract activity (nouns only). Summarize multiple processes in a single arrow.

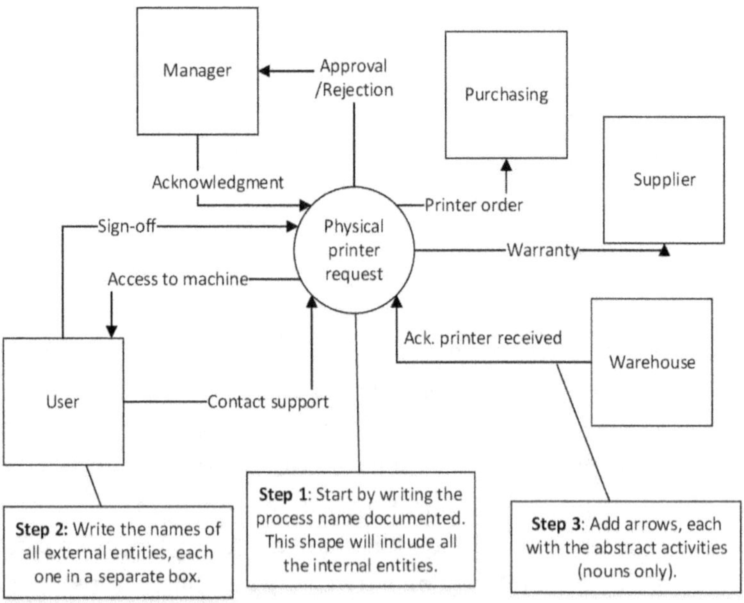

Figure 10 Context diagram example

Physical Data Flow Diagram (PDFD)

The physical DFD follows the exact steps cited for the activities list. A simple approach is to take the context diagram, remove the text from the internal entities (circles), and replace it with internal activities. The diagram should follow the top-down activities list data flow to avoid confusion. Instead of having a single circle with a physical printer request, the PDFD will have three (email system, IT support, and record system).

The physical DFD is more concerned with getting the final result delivered. This is how the system is implemented. In other words, if you are building software, each internal component of the PDFD will have at least one screen dedicated to it, and each external component will mean an integration point.

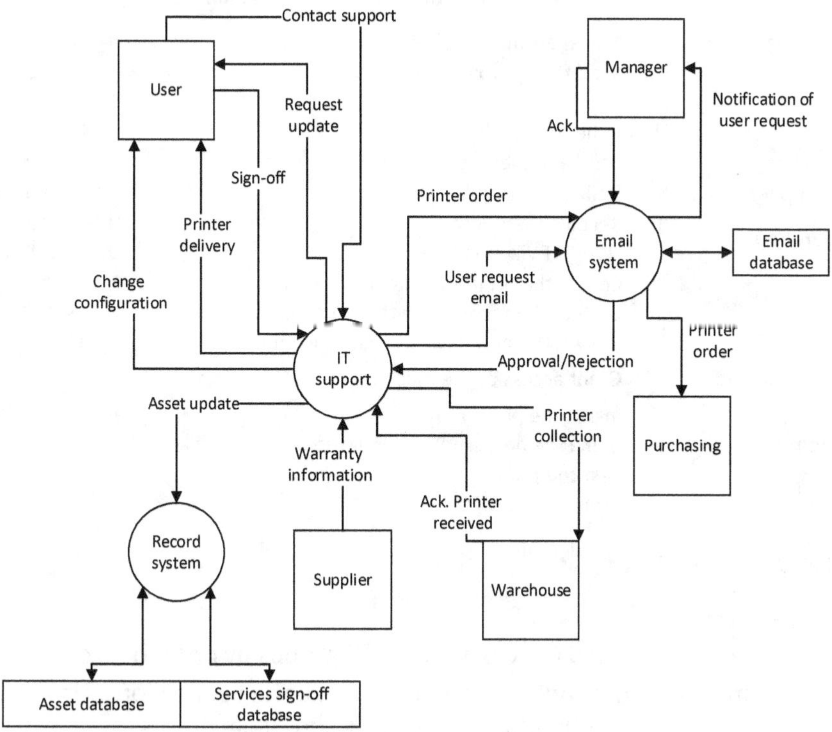

Figure 11 Physical DFD example

Logical DFD

The primary reason for building an LDFD is to extract the process and the system's business rules, and to indicate where the data should be coming from and stored. The purpose of the LDFD is to understand the inputs and outputs of the system. Typically, most of the LDFD is hidden from an end user.

The LDFD is a conceptual diagram that focuses on the activities and who is doing them. In this diagram, group activities are based on location and execution order.

Entities	Activities	Group	Group Name
User	1. Contact IT support	A	Receive request
IT support / helpdesk	2. Pick up the phone, read the email 3. Read/listen to the request 4. Write request approval from the user's manager	A A A	
Manager	5. Managers approve/reject	B	Approve workflow
IT	6. Send the approval to purchasing *or* Notify the user of the rejection	B	
Purchasing	7. Send a request to the supplier	C	Acquire printer
Supplier	8. Deliver the printer	C	
Warehouse	9. Receive the printer 10. Notify IT via email	D D	Deliver printer
IT support / helpdesk	11. Collect the printer from the warehouse 12. Update the record with the supplier warranty 13. Deliver the printer to the user's location	E E E	Install printer
User	14. Grant access to the machine	E	
IT support / helpdesk	15. Install the printer 16. Make the necessary configurations	E E	
User	17. Test the printer 18. Provide sign-off	E E	
IT support / helpdesk	19. File sign-off	E	

Table 4 Logical DFD groups

Now, after labeling A, B, C, D, and E groups by order of execution, start from the context diagram to make the connections. Use the table to link each lettered group with its circle.

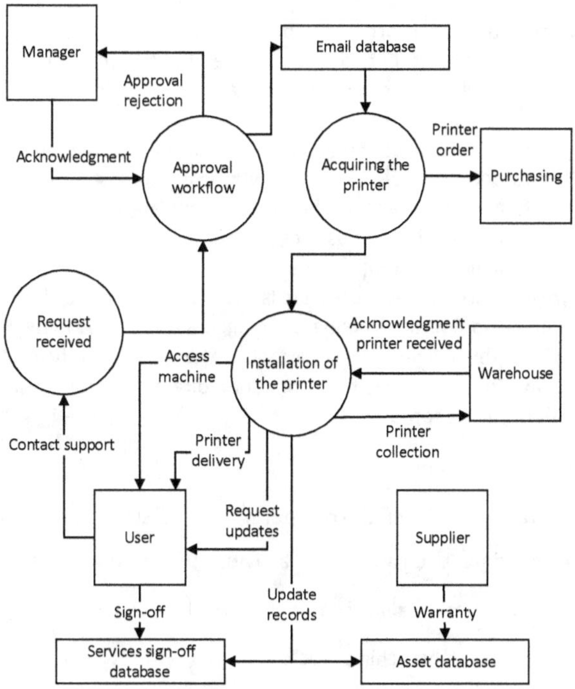

Figure 12 Logical DFD

Usually, PDFD and LDFD are used in the initial high-level stage or the initial statement of work or project proposal.

How to Draw a Flowchart

Before we begin, what are flowcharts, and how do they work?

What Is a Flowchart?

The flowchart represents the start and end of a process with some logic inside; it gives a picture of the steps necessary for specific actions from a particular actor or entity. So, in other words, it's one actor plus the system.

Flowchart Symbols

Table 5 shows the primary symbols used for flowcharts.

Symbol	Meaning
	**Start/end of the chart.** This symbol is the first and last symbol in any flowchart. It represents the start and end of the entire flow. Example: A call received from an end user can be the start, or an incident solved can be the end.
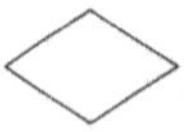	**Decision.** This is a yes/no question or true/false statement. This question's answers can be anything except a statement with the logic of true/false; this will ensure that all decisions are simple. Example: Did the previous steps solve the user problem? Yes, it will lead to the end path. Or no, it will direct to a different path.
	**Process/action.** This processing is usually done to input from another shape; it can be adding, subtracting, dividing, creating, or building. Example: Building the activity list or subtracting the price from the customer account.
	**Arrow.** This represents the connection direction between any two shapes. Usually, this is top-down.
	**A document** (a piece of paper).
	**A database or file on the computer**. Used to store data or retrieve data.
	**Output data.** Used after some activities that produce data.
	**Manual actions.** Calling someone or writing down something.
	**Subprocess**. A branching process.
	On-page/off-page connector. When drawing a complicated process, arrows end up going in all directions. This helps clean things up a bit; the circle on page is a reference on the same page (usually has a number to identify). The other shape is a reference to an off-page, in case the chart spans many pages (has a number on it to identify which reference).

Table 5 Flowchart symbols

Building a Flowchart

This may also be called a linear, swimlane, or cross-functional flowchart, depending on how many actors/parties/functions are involved. The name changes are variations of the same concept, but all types are generally called *flowcharts*.

There is a simple process I like to perform before I use the drawing tools to create the final flowcharts:

1. Get a flip chart, cut down the pages, and stick them on the wall. Consider each one a process page.
2. Write down activities and arrows on sticky notes. Ask available volunteers to move the sticky notes to the correct places. If you use an on-screen drawing tool instead, people

will look for the shortest path, an effort much harder than moving a sticky note.

3. Try to keep the flow as simple as possible. (Ask yourself if a 10-year-old can understand the flow. If not, simplify.)
4. Keep the details consistent throughout the entire map.
5. There should be no loops. If a problem is not fixed, don't start over and do unnecessary rework. Each action should involve several possible solutions. Alternatively, try to transfer the issue to a more specialized process. To avoid loops, add a decision with a count. (How many times has the system received a ticket ID, for example.)
6. Try to keep the flow in one direction, top-down or left-right. Don't point arrows in all directions. That adds confusion. (Remember, a 10-year-old needs to understand it.)
7. Add any shape, but include a diagram key to identify which shapes represent what.

Once all team members agree on a valid process, proceed with the actual flowchart using drawing tools.

Drawing Swimlane Charts

As a rule, if the entire process is performed by a single actor (entity), use top-down, traditional flowcharts. If there are many actors, use the *swimlane chart*. Likewise, if it's complicated, with many steps, use a swimlane to demonstrate the interactions between actors. For each actor, use a flowchart. Since our example is simple, we will use a swimlane to cover all activities. The swimlane flowchart is a repository for data from multiple flowcharts. It is based on internal and external entities from the physical DFD and the connections from the logical DFD. Entities can be vertical or horizontal, although vertical is preferred because it is easier to read. Typically, a swimlane chart is a high-level chart with lots of subprocesses. Each subprocess has its own flowchart.

If you find this overwhelming, I would advise you to start at a high level and then drill deeper whenever needed.

- **Level1**: This is called the block-based process. You can demonstrate the process at the first level in just a few steps, which is relatively easy. It's typically used to confirm the understanding *or* when you don't have enough time to build a complete process.

- **Level 2**: You take each block and break it down into more clear steps.
- **Level 3**: Take a block from Level 2 and break it down further.

Continue doing so until you reach the desired level of detail.

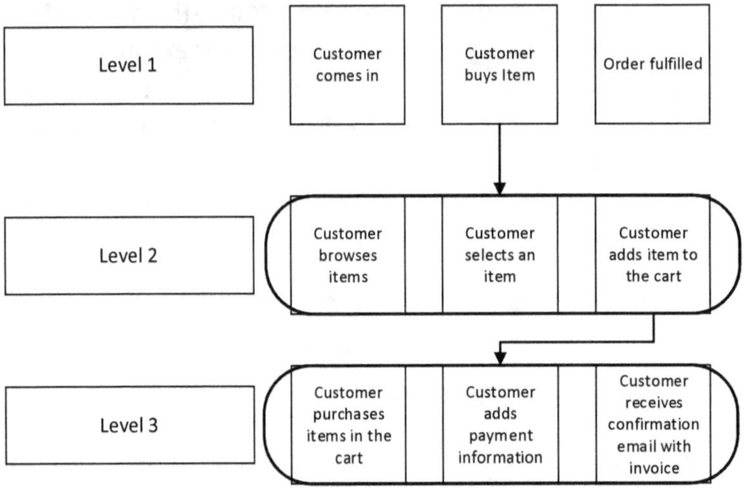

Figure 13 Process levels

Start from the highest concept, then take each step and drill deeper, breaking down the steps into more fine-grained steps. This is particularly useful in limited-time scenarios where there is a need to produce something fast. Some drawing applications have more attractive shapes than others, making a chart much easier to read and interpret. In this example, only basic shapes are used. The steps are as follows:

- Start by identifying the process, including its name and the owner's name.
- List all entities/functions/actors in the process.
- List all the activities based on their nature.

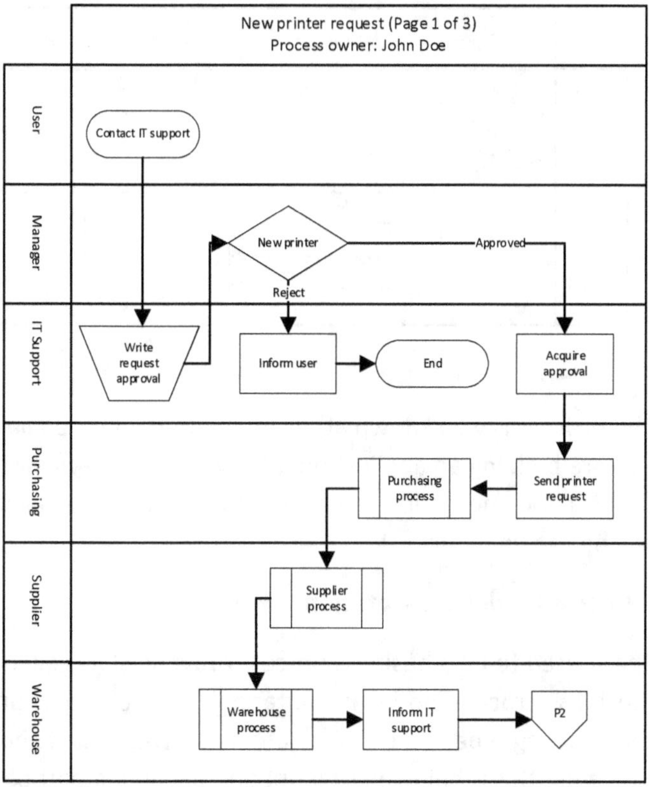

Figure 14 Flowchart page 1

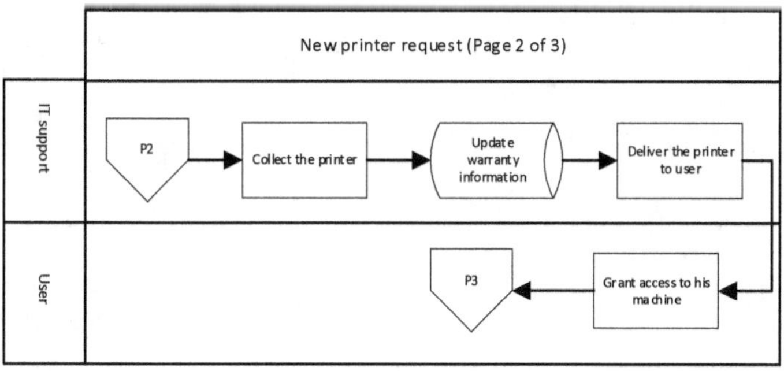

Figure 15 Flowchart page 2

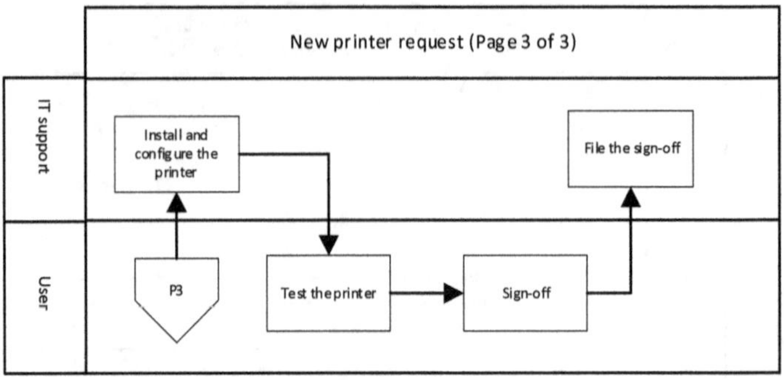

Figure 16 Flowchart page 3

The process is well known at this point, and you shed light on it. If you are building an application, this would be the final step. But if this is a documentation project to improve the internal process, this will be the first step.

Business Process Model and Notation (BPMN)

There used to be a business process drawing style called BPMN (business process model and notation). The computer understands this drawing type and can simulate it to determine its bottlenecks. However, this is being phased out and becoming part of the business process software package, not an independent element. Usually, this kind of software comes with a system engineer to operate the system. The BPMN is quite simple and almost the same as the flowchart.

Chapter 2: Models as a Requirement-Gathering Tool

You need to generate the initial design result and show it to the end customer to validate the overall understanding of what's been gathered. In any application, you have three main layers:

- Front end (view layer)
- Application (logic, business rule, access, and data retrieval layer)
- Database (data storage)

Regardless of the technology or development methodology, you will need these three components. Each layer is addressed through different diagrams and objects. However, most diagrams can be used in any layer. Usually, some diagrams are reserved for a specific layer. These diagrams can explain the layer in a much clearer way. Exploring these diagrams to understand which ones can be employed is essential to delivering the correct message.

As a business analyst (BA) or a product manager, part of the role is to define all three layers of requirements with the help of the subject matter experts, things like how the application will look, the business rules and restrictions, and finally, the database. This is considered an advanced topic for an analyst. But for a developer, this will be part of the high-level design diagrams in the project initiation.

Usually, the BA role defines the requirements and overview of the three layers a business application requires. Surprisingly, looking at the three layers will give you insights and highlight needs you did not address before. A specialized solution designer then takes this to the next level and adds more details. This means you will be interacting with three leading subject matter experts (SMEs):

- The UI/UX designer
- The developer
- The database admin or architect

Each of them will expect specific input from the initial requirements gathered to start designing the details of the solutions. Working with the customer to design the solutions is not an easy task. In doing so, the requirements will change or adjust, impacting the test cases and the project's output, so working with those SMEs will help achieve more accurate results. And to validate these results between the three parts of the triangle, you will need to use prototypes.

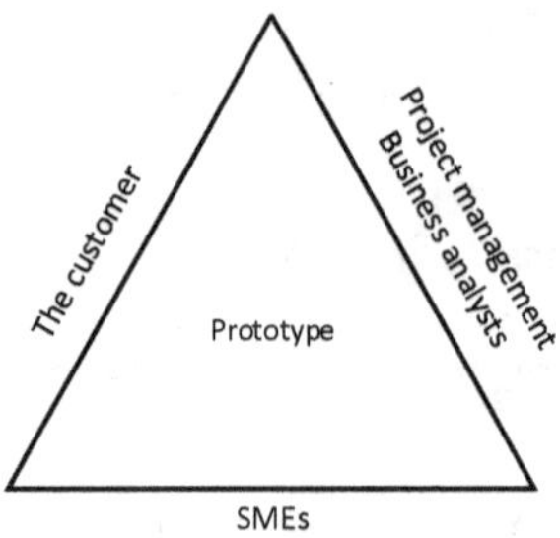

Figure 17 Prototyping

Prototyping is an approximation of the product or service. It is created to explore some aspects of the final product and ensure it matches the requirements and end-user specifications. Design sprints and prototyping differ slightly when creating the requirements. The primary difference is how to deal with uncertainty:

- The method of developing something new (innovation, not invention)
- Building on something familiar

It all comes down to the clarity levels and the starting point. Both processes are close, though when you don't have a clear vision, you need to perform the exploration phase to ensure you understand the requirements clearly.

Readers can begin at whatever stage is appropriate for their situations throughout this book. Nothing says if it's clear, you don't do more clarification. But in such a case, the returned marginal value will be minimal. This is the law of diminishing returns. You will often be adjusting an off-the-shelf application or pursuing a well-established application concept. So, uncertainty may be limited and quickly cleared. But if you have a high level of uncertainty, you will want some additional clarifications. This chapter explores the concepts of design sprints and prototypes. Each type is used in uncertain conditions—when creating a new application or something from scratch.

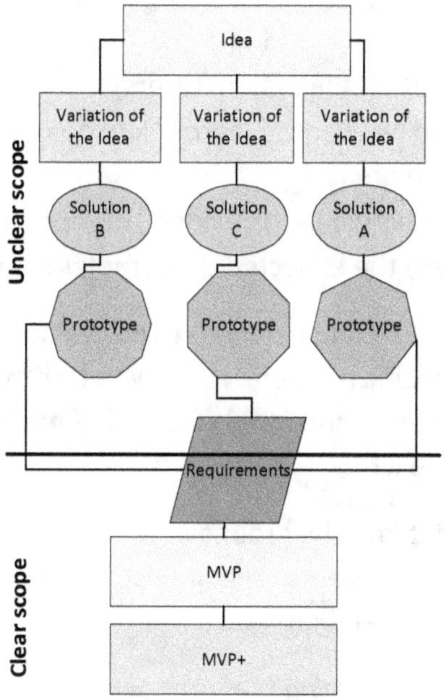

Figure 10 Uncertainty and scope

Executing the Sprint

In any given system, users may use only about 20 percent of the system daily. The remaining 80 percent is either used periodically or never (as in the case of packaged software). This means you can deliver business value from day-to-day operations from this 20 percent usage. This is faster than developing the whole software design and waiting for the value to be achieved. Deciding on what parts to create and what to defer until later is carried out in the design sprint. This design sprint approach was published in a book called *Sprint: How to Solve Big Problems and Test New Ideas in Just Five Days* by Jake Knapp et al., which primarily focused on creating a high-fidelity design in a week. So, integrating this method with prototyping for the entire software design across multiple layers, not just the interface, requires some adjustments.

The design sprint aims to identify who has what problem and then work jointly to solve it. The design sprint is specially made to develop a prototype that can help clarify what's required. In the design sprint, you need to know the answers to the following questions:

- Who is using the system (users)?
- What do we want to learn? How do our users deal with (problem areas)?
- Why we would like (the idea) + (improvement).
- What are the expected deliverables from this sprint?

The next step is to examine whether our value proposition is the best fix for a specific problem. Is it any better than the existing solutions? Are users motivated to use it? If not, how might they be motivated to use it?

The design sprint lays the groundwork for you to go to the customer with the ideas generated in the brainstorming workshops and query them on their likes and dislikes.

Full, or *native*, *prototyping* is another way to identify requirements and explore solutions. By showing users simple products, you can further recognize the additional features and requirements to enhance the product. Although this seems more practical than the design sprint, it costs more money and takes more time. So, by combining the two (design sprints and prototypes), you generate the maximum value with the lowest cost. Try first to launch the minimum viable product to collect feedback. Remember, you are exploring interaction with that 20 percent of the product users rely on for their day-to-day activities. The MVP will represent only about five percent of the full product. People usually overestimate their MVP. Start with what you think is your MVP, but realize that only about 25 percent of that is likely to be the actual MVP.

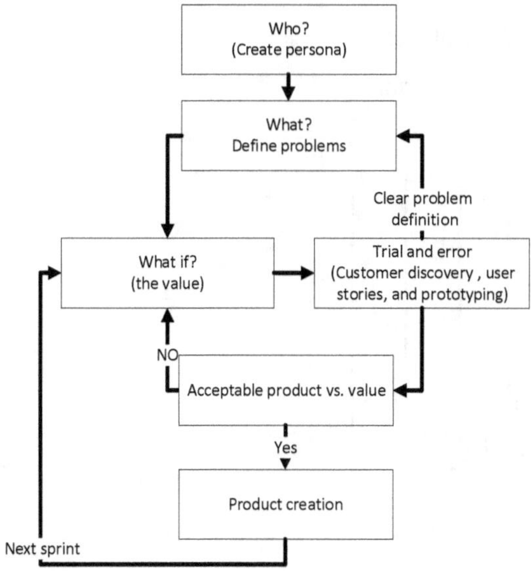

Figure 19 Design Sprint

The user interface is the first point of contact for the users, and in 70 percent of cases, it is one of the primary sources of user frustration. Try to work on this specific need early on.

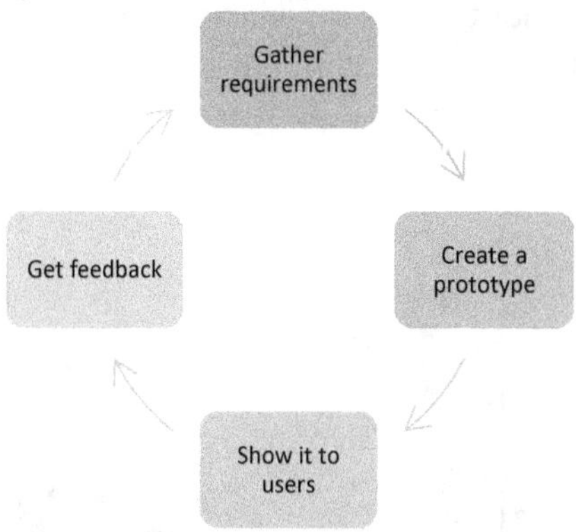

Figure 20 Design sprint and prototype cycle

Always do the prototypes in cycles, which typically consist of four steps:

- Gather requirements
- Create a prototype

- Show it to users
- Get feedback

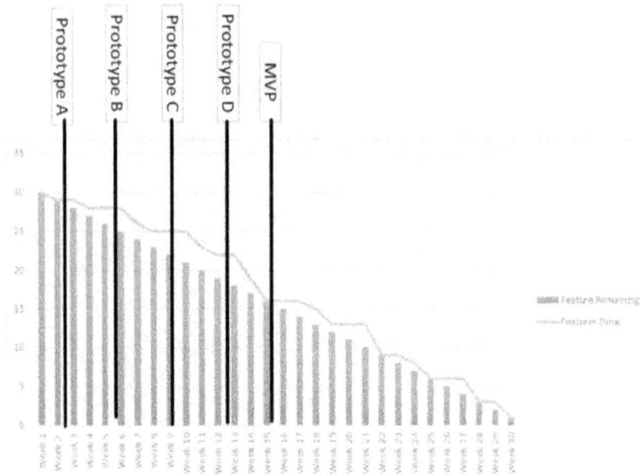

Figure 21 Prototype and burn-down

Usually, you perform this cycle repeatedly until no more requirements are needed to achieve your MVP. At this stage, the prototype should also have the full approval of the users. Typically, this occurs in three to four cycles.

Please note that this is a working prototype, not just a model (drawing). In other words, you modify the product with each change, enhancing it further as the project progress.

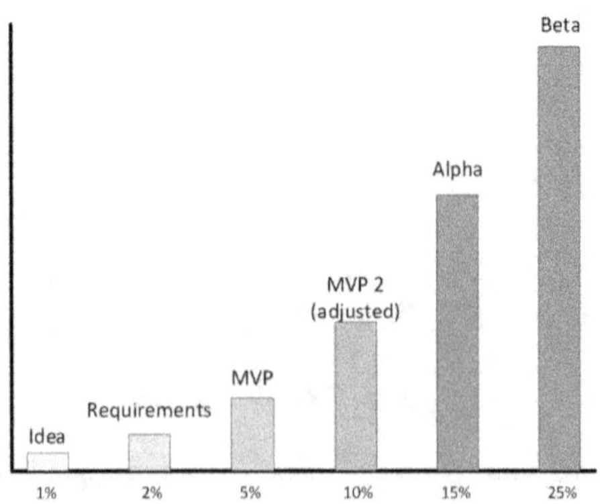

Figure 22 Features progress

In the next section, let's explore prototyping and how it might benefit the project.

Prototyping as a Tool to Reduce Rework

The primary role of the prototype is to elicit more feedback and fine-tune the requirements. Prototyping is an approximation of the product or service. The main benefits of prototypes are:

- **Learning (proof of concept [POC] model)**: explaining the usability and feasibility of a product
- **Communication**: Using a prototype to communicate design ideas effectively
- **Integration**: Prototyping subsystems and integrating them to test a complete system
- **Milestones**: Amassing achievements in the development process

Why Prototyping?

To reduce a specific type of uncertainty, and to reduce uncertainty in general, you can use many methods. The easiest way is to identify what you *don't* want first. Build things *you know will fail* somehow and test them out to collect feedback on the actual requirements. This way, the customer will point out things they like and dislike. But don't start with something very far off the initial requirement to avoid customer frustration.

Rapid Prototyping

Rapid prototyping is key to good solution design, something easy that can be made very quickly will help a great deal when building a product. Use a simple medium like paper or even 3D-printed objects. If off-the-shelf software is used, it could be the exact system but on a very small scale and adjusted with little to no configuration.

Rapid prototyping refers to the speed at which you generate the prototypes—especially the very basic ones. The number of issues discovered when you try to build a cardboard prototype, or even a sketch, will give insight into what will work, what won't work, and some of the challenges you can expect. Rapid prototyping can be critical to an idea's success, reducing the time required to build the product.

Ideally, you will generate ideas as quickly as possible to check their feasibility and ensure they are what the user wants.

The prototype doesn't need to cover everything, but it needs to cover a specific product aspect. Ideally, it would replicate the whole product, but the time allowed and feedback necessary usually require a much faster cycle than waiting for a full prototype. The trick is to generate ideas as quickly as possible. Check the idea's feasibility first and ensure this is what the user wants. Unfortunately, we get user feedback too late in the traditional process. You can build prototypes and show them to the end user using rapid prototyping. Since this is a prototype, the end user expects it to look unpolished. And they give you honest opinions quickly. So, it's okay to reveal the rough elements during prototype creation. You will discover ways to improve both the process and the product. It's an overall thinking exercise.

The prototypes are divided into multiple groups based on the information collected. The three types of prototyping that would be of interest are:

- Sketching and paper prototype
- Digital prototype
- Native prototype

You will need to go through each to build and validate your understanding.

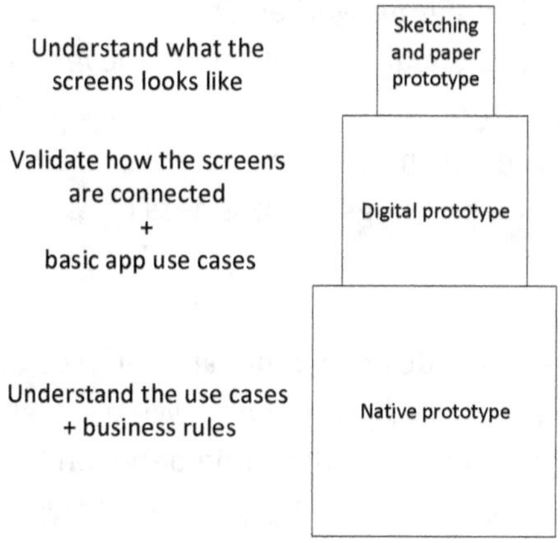

Figure 23 *Three levels of prototyping*

Usually, you start with the easiest (sketching and paper-based prototypes) and move to more advanced techniques during the project.

Sketching and Paper Prototype

The primary purpose of the paper prototype is to get an overall understanding of what the application's screens look like. In doing so, estimations of the effort required and sprint length could be made. This prototyping technique draws up the interfaces as they look to the end user. The sketch should evolve from a rough drawing to a realistic illustration.

The paper prototype depicts the application structure or user flow. Sketching will allow you to draw the ideas in your head with the minimum effort possible. It is needed to create a basic interface design, a basic application design, and, finally, a basic database design. In the next step, create a high-fidelity design. It's tempting to draw designs digitally, but try to flesh out as much of the idea as possible on paper. And having the ideas on paper will speed up the design work. You could also use paper prototype application kits (available online) to print/cut/glue to create a simple interface. It's also possible to use multicolor velcro in different shapes and sizes.

Paper prototyping also has another effect. It gets the correct feedback from the users. With finished prototypes, people will hold back because someone worked on it, and no one will want to devalue the work near completion. However, on paper, people will see that little effort was made and will give an honest opinion. This will assist in getting more requirements that were not even discussed before—things like business rules.

Digital Prototype

This is building an idea using digital interfaces to create an interactive experience for the user. We use digital-looking designs to ensure that the idea is the same between the customer and the SMEs working on it. This will give the prototype the same look and feel without building the actual software or final product. The outcome of digital prototyping is to understand how the screens are linked together and some of the use cases.

Native Prototype

Native prototyping uses real applications' data (sample data or demo data). This includes writing code in whatever language is used. People try to avoid these prototypes because they are very costly. We use them only if the customer is building something with many unknowns, like unknown integration points, or a new product that did not exist before. Native prototyping is used as a pilot to get better reactions from the customer on what's needed. The code in this prototyping is used to demonstrate the functionality. In other words, the SMEs will be taking shortcuts and the shortest path possible, which means:

- No clean code
- Simple use case
- Simple architecture
- Few or no nonfunctional requirements
- Little or no QA

This only needs to produce something that will function close to the expectation using everyday use cases. Afterward, fill in the special use cases and apply the best practices.

Let's start with a paper prototype and model the application interface.

Model Application Interface with the UI/UX Designer

This can be a simple drawing in any medium that shares a basic idea. This prototype is low cost and doesn't consume much time, although it focuses only on the general concept and an idea's look and feel. In the case of application development, there are two main parts—the front end and the back end. The front end is whatever the user sees, and the back end usually involves the database (sometimes middleware and the application as well). Let's explore how to build a user interface.

User Interface

The user interface (UI) has some industry standards to make it a viable product and save you lots of hassle when designing a sketch, mockup, or digital prototype interface.

What Is the User Interface?

It is the bridge between the content of a system or an application and the users, allowing the user to interact with it to get the desired output. The interface shapes the content and how to get to it and, in essence, shapes the experience. This means that the user interface drives the user experience (UX). Therefore, developing a better user experience requires adjusting the user interface. Any change in one will change the other.

- UI is usually focused on the visual design's structure and how to access the content.
- UX is focused on how a user experiences the user interface. The emphasis is on the story and user feedback.

The user interface design is the starting point, followed by the user experience designer, who adjusts the UI based on user feedback and prototype tests. The goal of adjusting the UI is to improve the UX. This is of little to no concern at this stage, however, since the primary goal is to build an acceptable UI and then improve it over time using a UX SME.

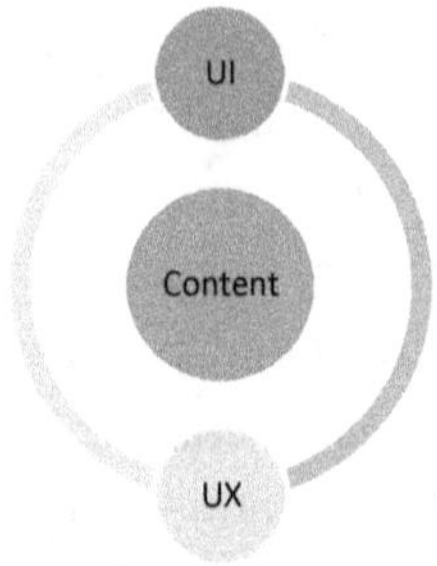

Figure 24 UI and UX

Now, what I call the front end is also divided into two segments:

- **Visible**: This includes the design elements and the look and feel of the site, usually done by a graphic designer.
- **Invisible**: This is the coding of the website, traditionally done by a programmer (CSS, JS, HTML, and so on).

What we will be discussing here is merely a part of the visible part, the placement of the graphics (not the actual graphics), and the input and output fields.

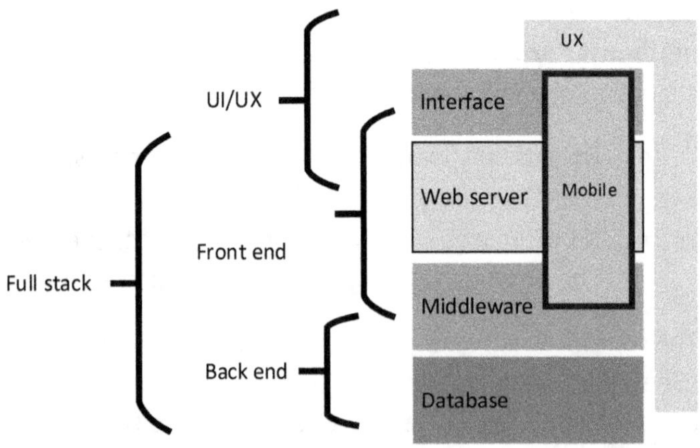

Figure 25 Full stack

Developing the user interface first will assist you in developing the application and the information needs because the interface clearly defines the information the end user/customer expects to be displayed and captured. To perform this process of prototyping the interface, you have to follow through with specific steps to make it as simple as possible:

- **Step 1**: **The site map** is extracted from the requirements you got earlier. This only exists to have some starting point. The site map is usually changed as you go along.
- **Step 2**: A **nonvisual prototype** is the initial capture of the screen requirements. You might even adjust the site map based on feedback. You jump between this step and the site map several times before moving ahead. You keep adding screens and changing the sitemap until no more adjustment is required (paper prototype).
- **Step 3**: **Wireframes**. Here you define each screen in a more precise way, using some drawing app (digital prototype).
- **Step 4**: **Mock design**. The purpose of mock design is to show how you will jump between screens and how the interface will function. You could use wireframes or sample photos from a stock photo site (smart digital prototype).

Site Map

Before building any prototype, create a site map depicting what screen leads to which other screens. This will allow you to determine how many screens are required in the application. The site map is created based on the initial understanding of the requirements, refined over time. To build it initially, get the requirements list and highlight two main requests:

- The input requirements (capture information, user required to insert some data)
- The output requirements (what information is expected to be displayed)

Once you determine these requirements, group them into screens. Please note that capturing and displaying on one screen is usually not a good idea. It used to be OK, but with the size of the mobile

Figure 26 *Site map*

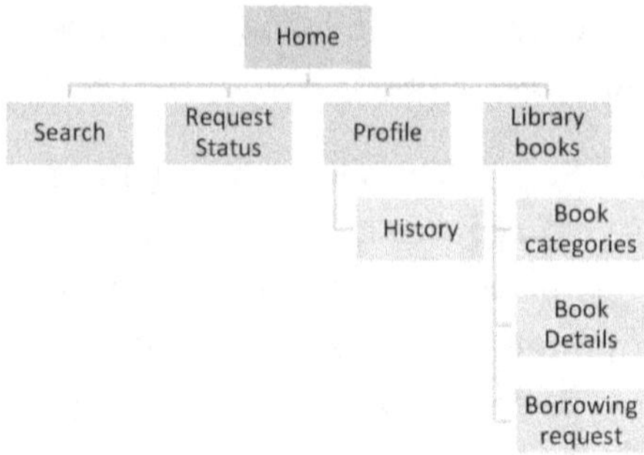

screen, it's better to make different screens initially.

A Nonvisual Prototype

Before building the visuals, plan on blank paper without any interface. During your meeting with the customer (user), you get a sticky note and sketch it or ask them to sketch it.

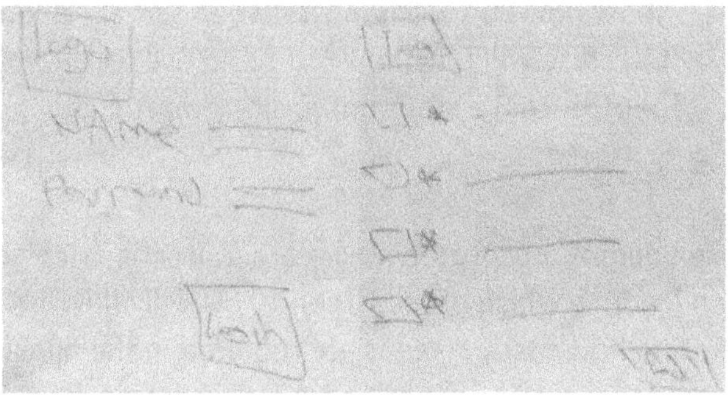

Figure 27 Nonvisual prototype

The benefit of this prototype is that it's real-time. You can develop it with the user to get their feedback immediately. This will highlight lots of missing or unclear areas in the requirements. After this step, it's expected to update the site map and the requirements lists.

Wireframe

With wireframes, the final look and feel will start to show up (in black and white). In this stage, ignore fonts and colors because adding the fonts and colors to the mix shifts the conversation from the functionality to the color and which one will look better. The primary concern is to lock the location created in the nonvisual prototype step. This ensures that every screen and clickable item is agreed on.

These mockups should not take more than an hour or so to make, so it's possible to create about 10 to 20 variations for each page in a single day. It's a basic nonfunctional representation of the product. It's used very early in the requirement-gathering phase. It lacks many design elements, and some don't even consider it a prototype. The squares with an X in Figure 28 represent a photo (clickable element or a button), and the gray boxes represent text. Using these simple elements will assist the stakeholders in articulating what they like and dislike.

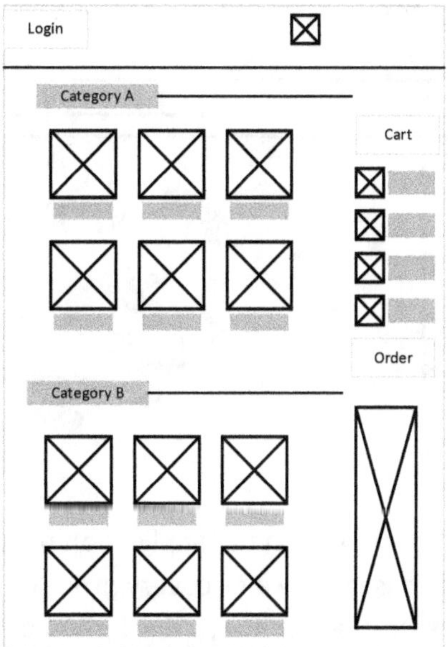

Figure 28 Wireframe

The simplest way to do wireframes (if you cannot draw) is to build a grid on a presentation slide (PowerPoint or similar application). Start by finding a website/application similar to the one you are trying to develop and snap the grid to ensure the proportions are correct.

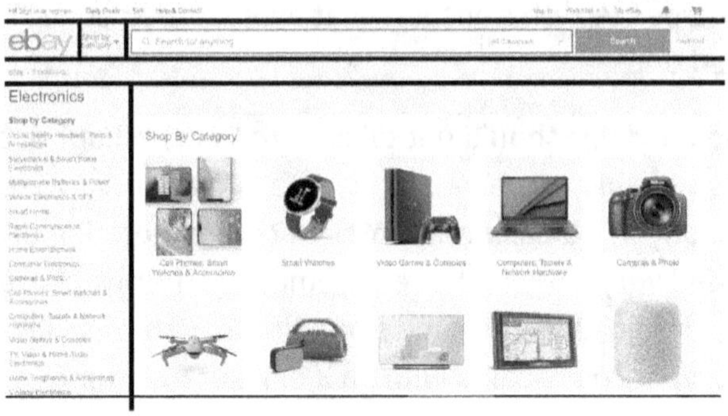

Figure 29 Site wireframe

After snapping the grid, delete the old photo; now this is the grid to start working on.

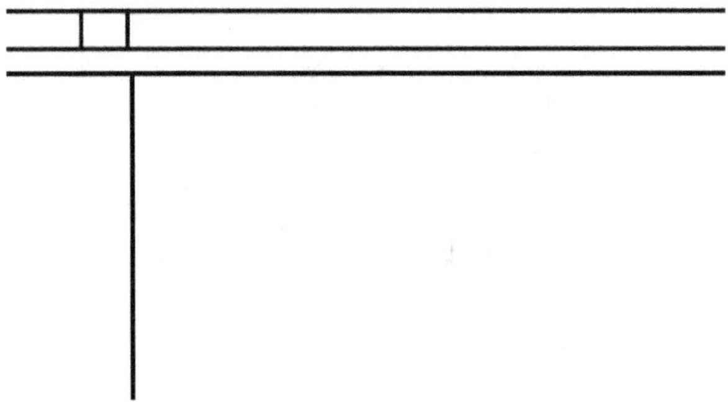

Figure 30 Wireframe skeleton

Adjust the frame to match the application being built. As mentioned, this is usually a discovery process, so you should experiment with lots of these to reach the best-fit design. Perform this process to avoid starting with a blank sheet because, for some people, it's quite challenging to start this way. But offering them a blank frame will generate better results and more variations.

Copying another application layout, though safe, is not recommended because it will make you fall into the generic trap, which means the website/application is already lost. You have to have a differentiator. Don't copy a layout. Start with a template or another website skeleton. If it looks like other websites after completion then you need to revisit the business drivers, but if it's not, this means creating something new, which is a key differentiator in any business. If you have a different value proposition, your value and the competitive edge will drive the interface and the experience to be different. Still, if you find out after all your work that you have a similar site/app to the competitors, then you will need to rethink your value add and have a more in-depth discussion with the business side in order to show the value more clearly on the app/site.

Use wireframes to demonstrate the pages and how they link, but I recommend deciding on the page's look and feel before mapping the pages. Look and feel plus mapping is where the mock design comes in.

Mock Design

Mock design shows the application's screens and how they interconnect with each other. This is different from the site map because this requires visuals as well. Never go for mock design without defining the majority of the requirements first because in mock design a single change might cause a significant effort to rebuild the screens and the connections between them. As mentioned earlier, there are two types of screens:

- Input screen: used to input data (capture data)
- Display screen: used to display data

Start with the login screen (input screen) and the application's home page, and then each element of the home screen can lead to another page, which links back to an icon on the home screen. Do so until mapping out the entire application. Consider the application simple if it includes fewer than 30 screens, and complex if it has around 80-plus screens. Although this is subjective based on the application functionality, it's one of the general indicators.

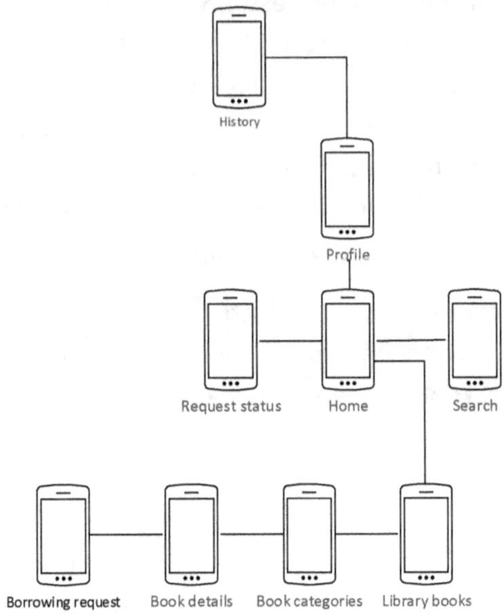

Figure 31 Mock design

Presentation Tools

The best way to design more complex prototypes is by using special software. You can create and link pages to each other to simulate a functioning app. This software will make some sort of digital prototype. Alternatively, you can do it manually by printing out the screens and simulating their functions as if the user were pressing them. There will be a bit of a learning curve for the user in understanding why they will be pressing a button on a piece of paper, but such a method, although crude, may be surprisingly effective and efficient.

At this point, I have to include a warning. If you design it too well, the customer will think the application/website is ready for use, so always set expectations that this is only a design interface.

A common application for creating wireframes is Balsamiq. It's the easiest tool to use when creating wireframes, and it's not that expensive. If you wish to link screens to create some sort of interaction and digital prototype, inVision freehand is one example of such software. It's easy to use and generate models. Adobe XD is the most feature-rich application in this area, but the downside is that it requires some design skills to operate, unlike the other two. I have also found Figma to have a good balance between technical needs and simplicity.

General Best Practices for Great UX You Should Consider

After you finalize the initial interface mockups, please go through the following list to confirm that it applies to the interface:

1. **Templates design** considers the template a starting point because of its familiarity and because it's content agnostic. But plan to have to adjust and fit the application content.
2. **Responsive design** is the ability to adapt to the display screen. For example, the website might have three columns on a PC, but only two on a tablet, and maybe only one on a phone—the design changes based on the device.
3. **Information design** presents lots of data in an easy-to-understand format. This is used for a website with lots of information or very complicated reports. Unfortunately, this one is based on the prototype you will have. Experiment to get the best feedback from users. The design should be based on the data types and the content volume.
4. **Excellent user interface design**: You should be following what's called *heuristic evaluation* (there are many templates to follow online), but every screen should pass the following checklist:
    - **Something familiar**: Something that the users are used to in their day-to-day lives, and know-how to operate.
    - **Action/feedback**: Whenever the user does something, feedback must happen.
    - **Consistency across all the systems**: If a button looks like another button, it should function the same way. The same applies to colors and icons.
    - **Intuitive and straightforward**: It should not need special training to use or operate. If this is impossible, it should have just a few interactions to learn how it works.
    - **Undo/redo and autosave**: The user needs to feel safe—and no action should impact them without a final confirmation, and if they make a mistake, they can always go back and fix it. Also, the user needs to be able to stop working and

resume from that point forward without filling everything in again.

- **User-familiar language**: Try to use the user's language, not technical language.
- **Clean and functional design**: Avoid design that is not functional, for example, a flashing screen or too many elements on one screen.
- **The maze**: Avoid having more than three levels, ideally no more than one main menu and two submenus.
- **Freedom**: Allow the user to move in any application direction—forward, backward, and save.
- **Flexibility**: The application should be flexible and allow the user to adjust things as the user sees fit (like customizing the interface).
- **Recognition over recall**: The user should know a function when they see it, without having to reference a manual.
- **Show status**: The application should show the current status, like saving (the spinning beach ball or the hourglass).
- **Prevent errors**: Every user now expects a message saying "do you wish to continue?" when they press *cancel*. To avoid deleting the user's work by mistake, you have to ask such confirmation questions.
- **Gray out unavailable options early on**: Don't offer users options that will give errors later on in the process. For example, don't allow booking of an unavailable time slot. Prevent that by graying out the unavailable time slots at the beginning of the process.

Though these are considered nonfunctional requirements, they will impact the application design, for example, temporary autosave, forward/backward, and so on. Though these things might seem simple, they significantly increase the overall positive customer experience.

Prototype Testing and User Feedback Capture

In prototyping, it's always "quantity over quality." Produce quickly, regardless of the quality, and learn from the mistakes. In other words, when doing a wireframe, you don't do just one; instead, build three or more, then let the customer select one and tell you why they like it and why they dislike the other ones. This articulation from the customer is one of the primary objectives of the prototypes. The more variations you can make, the better. Though this is considered waste, wasting half a day at the start of the project is way better than wasting a month doing rework. The mistakes will accumulate quickly to present progress and a hockey stick curve. Focusing on prototype quality will result in one or two prototypes and not generate as many insights.

You can perform prototyping in two ways—either serial or parallel. Try a mix of both to maximize efficiency. Start with many parallels and show them to the users (variations). The next step is to start collecting feedback and determining which ones the users liked better and why. And if they disliked something specific, this should also be considered. Over time, try to incorporate these elements into one branch and perform more complex serial prototyping.

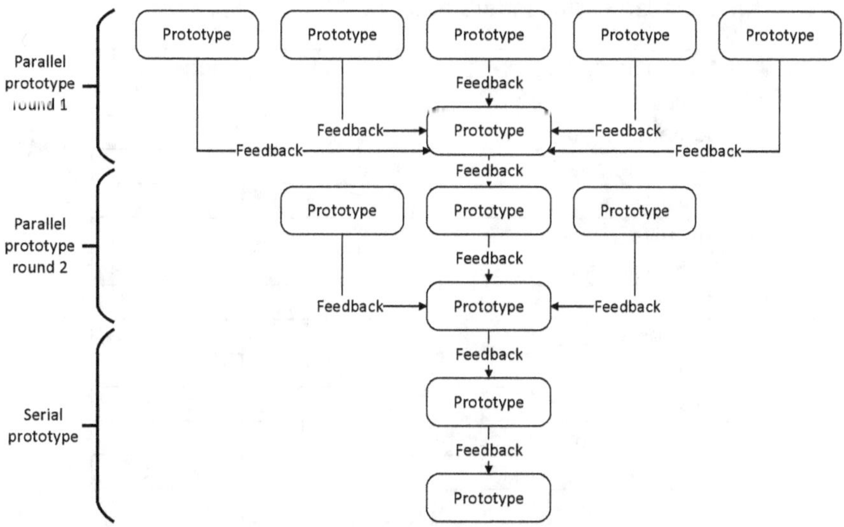

Figure 32 Prototype testing

Another critical aspect of having multiple prototypes is separating the ego from the actual feedback. If someone has one idea, it becomes their representation, and they don't accept criticizing it and will try to defend it and convince others of it. But if there are multiple ideas, they will learn more and become inclusive of all feedback. So, it's good to generate more ideas by asking the team to contribute to the concept before it becomes the main branch of the prototype.

Collect Feedback

The more you show the prototype, the more feedback is collected. It's accepted for 70% to 80% of the issues to be discovered prelaunch. But it's a matter of cost and time. The golden range is three to seven testers. After that, a discovered issue is likely particular to a specific user group or use case.

You are scoring against the general best practices. Give each tester a scoring sheet (or heuristic evaluation template) and let them fill it out and leave comments. You don't have to use all the mentioned items of best practices. Use the things that matter to the stakeholders. Also, name the scoring sheet to represent something the user can easily understand.

Screen name (ID):	Rating 1 to 10	Notes
Something familiar		
Action/feedback		
Consistency		
Intuitive		
Undo/redo and autosave		
Familiar language		
Functional design		
Freedom		
Flexibility		
Recognition over recall		
Show status		
Prevent errors		
Gray out unavailable options		

Table 6 *Feedback collection form*

Once you finish all the tests, list the comments and note with which feature and in which step problems happened. Don't forget that you are also collecting comments about user actions noticed during the test. For example, suppose you saw a user hesitate on a specific screen. This could indicate a confusing UI, so note it for further development. If many users hesitate on the same screen, it's not intuitive enough.

Testers and Feedback

Don't confuse this undertaking with user acceptance testing (UAT). In this case, testers do not follow a script. Instead, you present a screen with one brief sentence or paragraph about an application and have users explore it by clicking through it freely.

- In the paper prototype, you would pretend they are clicking through it freely, with minimum interaction or explanation from you.
- You would give the link on a device if you made a digital prototype.

If they notice something missing, note that missing item. The general idea is to let users play and test the experience in a very free-form way. Make notes on the heuristic evaluation form for every screen the users comment on.

Figure 33 Optimal number of testers

Final Thoughts

Do you have to worry about all of this from the start?

The answer is yes and no. This is just a tool in the tool kit to develop a better application. Since most of the changes happen in the interface layer, it's good to lock these requirements early in the project. In other words, it's not an official business analyst responsibility, but it's simple and will greatly help. So, my advice is if you can clarify requirements from the beginning, try to do it. If not, stick to the templates and evolve from that point.

The UX designer usually goes beyond what we discussed here. Still, these fundamental elements need definition to deliver the application smoothly. Later on, things like navigation, buttons, sidebars, and menu positioning are explored more by the system's UX designers. If you have a UI/UX designer, this will be great, but if you don't (and this is often the case in many companies), what's discussed here can at least allow for a better application or website.

Chapter 3: Model Application with the Development Team

If you do not get the functionality right, no amount of design (UI and UX) will solve the issue. So, focus on the functionality, not the interface or the experience. Those come later, after the functionality. Many requirements fall through the cracks during project execution or are simply forgotten. To avoid this, you need to build and map the requirements directly to the application design. Because when designing, the conditions might change, for example, small changes that will reduce the time to implement or adjust feature prioritization.

Some prefer to go straight to a concept map/diagram to keep track of the requirements since it's simpler to build. Concept diagrams are very similar to the mind map explained earlier. But, though it's a great brainstorming tool, it's not a design diagram, and it could get messy. Unless you have a clear mapping of the requirements to a specific function in the application, this could lead to unclean code and a nightmare when having to change something. So, using models instead of simple mind maps or concept maps is strongly recommended. But when it comes to technical diagrams (models), there are two possibilities:

- You are a business analyst with little coding experience or no coding skills.
- You are a developer with experience in coding.

The business analyst will like the models lightweight, while the developers will want them verbose. This is an overlapping area between the developer and the BA. However, there is still a big difference in drawing details. Still, the overall idea should be understandable for both. As a BA, start with the lightweight version of the diagrams. Then during the project, the developer will add the necessary details to these diagrams. Adding all of these details at the beginning of the project is not required. Start with the business skeleton (to ensure that the business users understand it) and then hand it over to the SMEs to add all the necessary details.

The same applies if you are a developer. When developing these diagrams, start with the basic business language. Please don't get too technical and then try to explain it to the business users. Classes, attributes, operations, message types, and return values are considered technical. The business users will be lost and might agree to something they don't fully understand. Then you will be getting one change request after another, or worse, the customer will not accept the project. Start with basic business language, and once you get agreement, feel free to add all the technical language and documentation you require.

Before you start, you need to understand how the programming impacts the models and the whole process.

How Programming Languages Impact Design

The style and the design should follow one of three main development styles that will influence which diagram would be most beneficial. Modifying and debugging the application is nearly impossible without following one specific style. It's a matter of how to organize the code.

Structured programming: This focuses on the code's structure, subdividing the code into functions for easier analysis (procedural programming). Start by defining a problem, breaking it down into simple tasks/functions, and then address these tasks, thus creating a hierarchy of tasks to complete to solve the problem. For large programs, it's possible to implement a modular approach in which each module contains all the needed information for it to function. It becomes a separate program to solve a specific issue, and calls on another program module. This module will require specific input from the one before it and will produce the exact output for the following module.

Object-oriented programming: An object combines data and function, allowing for things like encapsulation (hiding data and functions from other objects) and inheritance (allowing separate objects to have a similar group of variables and functions).

Function programming: The code is divided into generalized functions (not hard coding input in them) and relies on variables to execute.

Each has its own set of languages and tools, and support groups as well. How the code is organized will allow and disallow the usage of some diagrams. For example, a class diagram is quite challenging to draw in functional programming. In contrast, sequence and timing diagrams could be very beneficial.

There are three ways to use models; some diagrams can be used across all three layers, and some can be used in just one:

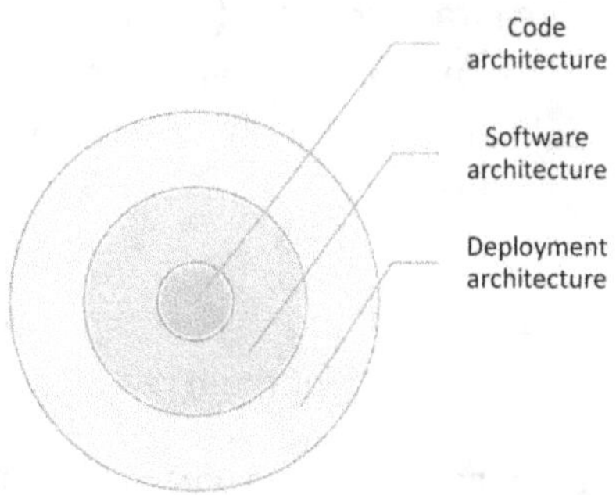

Figure 34 *Ways to use models.*

- Layer 1: Code architecture (OOP, FP)
- Layer 2: Software architecture (monolithic, SOA, microservice)
- Layer 3: Deployment architecture (servers, containers, database systems, networks, and so on)

Each level represents a specific way of drawing the diagram. Combining this with the three development styles mentioned will generate many variations. Though most diagrams mentioned can fit with any of the three, some will be very beneficial, shedding light on some aspects of a problem. A timing diagram, for example, is very valuable in microservices to determine the timeouts.

I am basing these diagrams on the unified modeling language (UML). UML is a Waterfall-based paper design used years ago. I am repurposing it to create a common baseline. The common word baseline means it has common grounds (assumptions and definitions), so anyone who reads it can understand it clearly. This is sometimes called a conceptual model containing the items and their relationships.

When we use the word *model*, we usually mean a representation of something. Based on the model used, this representation can be abstract or very detailed. It can be representative of one part of the overall. Again, it will be based on which type of model will be used. Modeling is the visual representation of the system that will be developed; it helps the client and the developer understand the potential errors or bugs in the application. For many software companies, the strategic cost of software increases due to technical debt. And with that, time to develop the software also increases. Modeling could help reduce the cost and time by reducing the rework and the duration.

Why Modeling?

A model is required for four main reasons:

- To build consensus on what the project or the software will look like and remove personal assumptions
- To ensure you better understand what's required and what the final product functions look like
- To document a complex system and show different aspects of this system
- To test out the potential system interactions without developing the needed code (it's considered a form of a prototype)

The model's primary use cases are:

- Visualizing a project (in planning and high-level design).
- Prototyping a project (the execution of a project).
- Documenting a project (as a deliverable of a project).
- Problem analysis. Suppose you have a software issue but don't understand where it originated. In that case, you can draw it to understand the situation better.

This means modeling is not a development method, and it's for everyone to visualize. It can be used on any system, software or otherwise. A physical system can also have diagrams, like state machine diagrams.

The diagram may consist of actors, processes, classes, or functions. A diagram helps software engineers understand the system or application they are developing. Documenting software or a system application plays a crucial role as the developer or programmer formulates the idea of the software application they will develop.

Note: Because many charting vendors are out there, they keep trying to differentiate themselves by inventing new diagrams, but the concept is the same.

Types of Modeling Diagrams

There are many types of diagrams, but based on their functions and structures, they fall into two major categories.

Structural Diagram

The structural diagram describes the inner structure of the system software. It represents the building components, the relationship between the actors/users, classes and modules, and the parts of the system. The primary concern of all the structural diagrams is to explain the system's components, not how the system functions. Let's take a more straightforward example. In our example, let's look at something familiar. The human foot has many bones, which are the building blocks of the foot.

Bones of the Human Foot

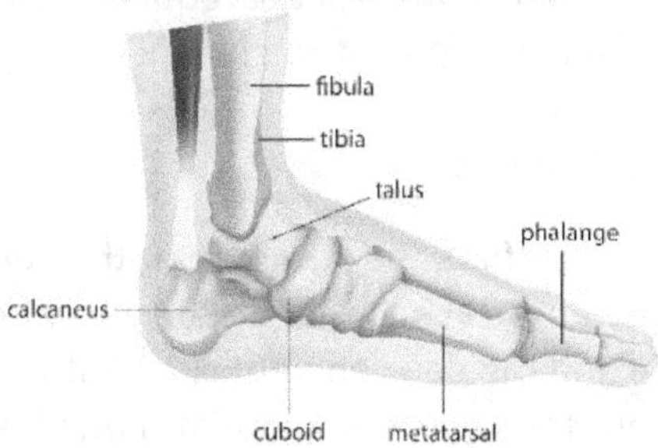

Figure 35 Bones of the human foot

Knowing the building blocks does not cover what you can and can't do with the elements mentioned (how to move them). It's a static view of the component and how each part fits together. This is a structural diagram.

Behavioral Diagram

In terms of our previous example, these diagrams explain how you can move your foot and what you can and cannot do. Each diagram explains a certain aspect, like how things connect while moving or the possibilities and range of movement. As you might have guessed, there may be hundreds of such diagrams—the same for a complex system. Hundreds of options exist to depict the system's possibilities. It's possible to cheat when creating these diagrams by making the system less flexible and reducing both the number of parts and the possibilities. Over time, add details to make it more flexible.

For example, start with a wooden puppet with limited possibilities and add details as you move along. This helps to reduce the overwhelming feeling you will get at the beginning of the project and facilitates creating an MVP.

Figure 36 Wooden puppet

Though this will not include all the required details, building an MVP will simplify the development road map.

Which Diagram Should You Use?

Now, which comes first, the structure or the behavior diagrams? The short answer is the one that will be easily understood by your business side and the development side. Both types will impact each other, but try to adopt a spiral format, alternating between both types of diagrams, to avoid running out of time because you allowed too much time for one type. Also, please note that not all diagrams are necessary to code an application, so select the best for

the situation. Building the models is quite time-consuming, so at least use one from each group as a rule of thumb.
The common case that usually causes many issues is that the group creating the diagrams is the development team, acting as the business analysts. The development team is usually more interested in the technical diagrams (like class, object, and use case), or they've plugged too much technical info into the business diagrams. Or worse, they did not do any diagrams.

Modeling diagrams should be straightforward, except for the end-of-project documentation. The primary objective of these diagrams is to get *other* nontechnical groups on board the software project. This is why you need to be aware of the software stakeholder's audiences.

Build the Models to Reach Maximum Value for the Audience

Each of the diagrams is considered some simple prototype. Each one sees the system differently. Each of them expands the overall understanding of different system parts. For example:

- The timing diagram will make you consider the duration of the object in memory and the load time on any given server.
- The deployment diagram will make the deployment with system engineers as simple as possible.
- The communication diagram will make life easier for the security team because they now understand which system is talking to which system and why.
- The sequence diagram will make life easier for the business and the governance team.
- The components and package could also help in designing the containers of the application (the K8 or similar application cluster deployment).

As you might have noticed, the audience for these diagrams will vary greatly. It's not only the SMEs of the system but also other groups. The returned value is high from all of these diagrams, but the challenge I always see is time. As mentioned, each diagram targets a specific something, and they vary in the type of details because of the same reason (the audience for them is different). So, let's take a closer look at the audience for these diagrams.

For any given software solution, you have the following audiences that would be interested in your software:

1. The business team (the rules of the business and the flow of the process)
2. The development team (how they will take all the requests and code them)
3. The system engineer team (how they will deploy this code into the server while maintaining the performance of the servers from the aspects of the resources)
4. The security team (how to secure this software)
5. The GRC team (how this software will meet the legal and regulatory requirements)
6. The network team (the communication and bandwidth requirements of this application)
7. The UI/UX team (how the system will be user-friendly and enhance the user's experience while maintaining the branding)

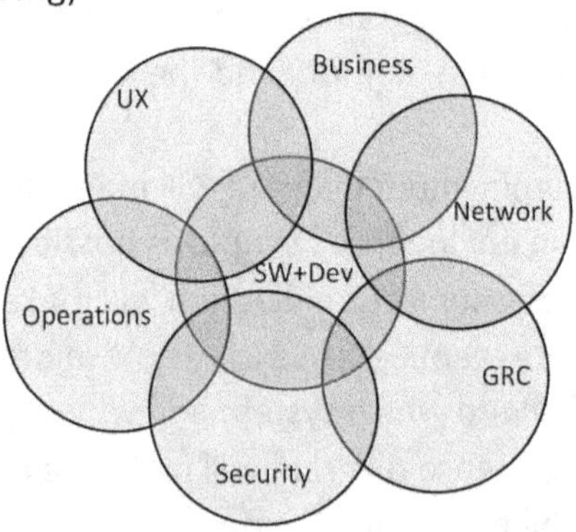

Figure 37 Software operations stakeholders

So, based on the project and the audiences, you will have three levels of diagrams:

- **Core**: Without these, SMEs can't develop the application.
- **Additional diagrams**: These diagrams explain a specific aspect of the software.

- **Extra**: These diagrams are necessary, but their use is specific to particular use cases, so use them as needed.

How to Build Application Models

Due to the nature of Agile development, you don't have full visibility of the overall structure of the system. So instead, focus on the required functions and features. In other words, the flow of the system. The starting point for that is starting with building the decision tables, which represent the gates to move from one status to another.

Decision Tables

Though this is not a diagram, I have found it very helpful in modeling the what-if scenarios. It's used when many factors dictate a decision or a path. It's best to create them to identify all the scenarios that will lead to either *yes* or *no* status. It's best to have a decision table for each of the statuses. Tweak the table to fit whatever scenario is needed, but in the end, don't go directly to drawing; otherwise, things will quickly get very complicated.

So, start with the simplest form of the decision table (a one-factor status question), then drill deeper and create a special table that governs more complicated decisions or states.

State	State valid	State invalid
Electricity on	Correct voltage	Very low voltage
Electricity off	No power below the minimum voltage	Above minimum voltage

Table 7 *Decision table for a lamp*

For each state in the table, build an advanced state table to determine the possible conditions for that state. So, as a best practice when creating advanced tables:

- Use only yes/no questions (not values because values should be part of the condition).
- Keep it limited to four or five factors. If you need more, create a new table since this is a basic probability. The more columns you have, the more options you will get

(5^5=25 scenario, 4^4=16 Scenario, 3^3=9 scenario). Note how a single column added increases the number of scenarios significantly.

	From 1 to 50 unit	1000+ unit?	Is it a local city?	Decision
1	Yes	No	No	Yes
2	No	Yes	No	No
3	No	No	Yes	No
4	Yes	Yes	No	Yes

Table 8 Decision tables example

Decision tables are the governance of the application, or what your application needs to do. Typically, this is extracted from business rules. Once finalized, move to describe the static components of the application.

Structural Diagrams

You will need to pick at least one from the structural group, though both are highly recommended.

Class Diagram

The class diagram provides an overall sketch of a software system by showing the classes, attributes, operations, and relationships. It consists of three parts: class name, attributes, and operations. It plays an important role in software application development by helping in constructing the code. The class diagram gives you an idea about the type of objects existing in the system and their relationship. You can consider a *class* as a group of characteristics defining a specific data processing set in the system. It offers a high-level view of an application. This modeling methodology applies to almost all object-oriented methods.

Why Do You Need a Class Diagram?

In the case of monolithic applications where both application and data access logic are combined inside the user interface, the use of the class diagram is almost zero. However, today's software developers have shifted toward component-based applications that have the flexibility to be maintained, extended, and scaled from the desktop to the cloud. These applications require the creation of classes with boundaries and a balanced distribution of responsibilities. This is where class boundaries can help. It enables the design of classes, which become the building blocks of the application.

Class diagrams enable the documentation of class structure (operations and attributes). They also play an essential role in understanding relationships between classes, inheritance hierarchies, and responsibilities of the entities that provide the system behavior. The primary usage of the class diagram is system planning and design. A typical application has multiple classes. But nowadays, most applications already have the classification premade. Or it's possible to find them online (Stack Exchange network, for example), which means, in most cases, most things are defined for the application because someone somewhere thought of something similar. And you only have to reference them in the class diagram. As mentioned, a class diagram is a planning tool used to ensure you prototype the classes and application layout correctly.

The class diagram forces you to think about classes and even reduce them. Some tools allow generating many classes with very simple steps. But this will result in duplication in code, and it's just bad practice. If you choose the easy path, you might even have to do code refactoring to solve an issue later. The same issue will happen if the application has only a few classifications. One code class might have way too much power over the others, which is not good.

Pros and Cons of the Class Diagram

Pros:

- Class diagrams provide a blueprint of the application or software that a programmer is going to structure.
- It makes coding easy (it builds a road map for SMEs).
- It shows the instances and functions of a class.

Cons:

- Understanding a class diagram requires technical knowledge.

- It gets difficult to understand a class diagram if a software application has many classes.
- It takes a lot of time to draw a class diagram.

Parts of the Class Diagram

Vital elements of the class diagram are:

- Class name
- Attributes
- Operations

Class Name

The name is written in the top segment. A class is a blueprint of an object that can share the same semantics, relationships, operations, and attributes. The class is portrayed as a rectangle that consists of a name, attributes, and operations in their respective compartments.

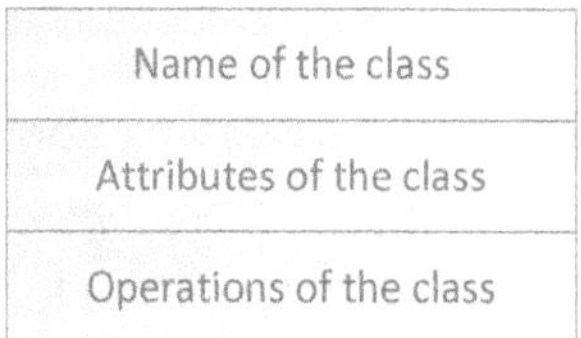

A box with three partitions represents classes in a class diagram. These partitions should include the following:

- **The name of the class** is in the top partition.
- **Attributes (variables)** are usually in the middle partition.
- **Possible operations (functions)** associated with a class will be in the bottom partition.

Attributes

The named property of the class explains the object being modeled. For example, your name and age are attributes of yourself. They only define things that differentiate yourself from another person. If all the elements have the same attributes, removing them is OK because they will be null and waste data space.

Attributes are placed in the compartment below the class name. An attribute that is computed from other attributes is called a *derived attribute*. For example, if you give me your birth date, I don't have to ask you for your age, as it can be computed easily. So, age, in this case, is called a derived attribute. Here are some of the characteristics of attributes:

- They usually are written along with the visibility factor.
- The accessibility of an attribute of a class is described by its visibility.
- The names of the attributes should be meaningful.

The four visibilities are public, private, protected, and package, denoted by +, –, #, or ~ signs, respectively. These are the signs in front of the attributes.

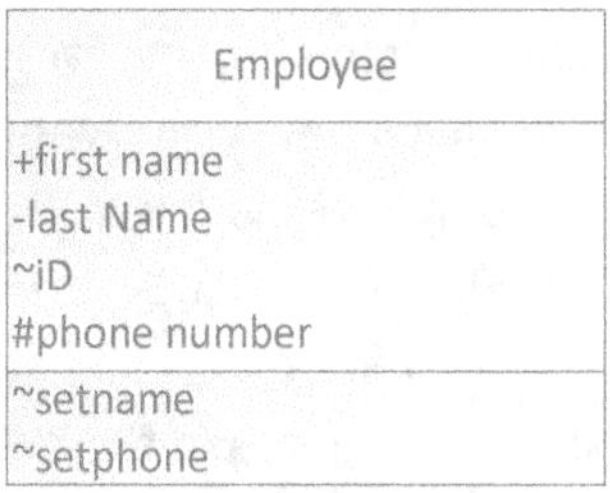

- The – sign means this is a private attribute; no one else can access it. For example, an employee's social security number.
- The + means something public that any other class can access. In this case, the first name and email might be public and OK to be seen by everyone.
- The # means the attribute is protected, which means it can be accessed by the same class or subclass. In our example, the group or department would have visibility to the employee photo, but no other departments would be able to see the photo.
- Lastly, the ~ means the package (the other parts in this layer of the application) would have visibility to the attribute.

Another example of visibility is assuming your information is class as per our previous example. The private sign means the confidential information you don't wish to share with others, like your passwords or credit card number. The public sign means things you are OK to share with anyone, such as your height; since anyone can see it, it's considered public. The protected sign means something you want people around you to know, but you don't wish everyone to know it; this could be your first name and last name. The tilde means one step bigger, like your community knowing your first name only or last name only.

Now for the attributes' left side, you should specify the data types. The most common are:

- **Integer**. A positive number.
- **Floating-point number**. A number, but used only when your numbers are counting in millions, for example, numbers like how many km or miles between us and the sun. This is used to simplify the number by removing a specific base—for example, to change 0.00000000001 to .01—in order to do more straightforward calculations.
- **Character**. This is used to make the data cleaner, but is rarely used.
- **String**. Traditionally a sequence of characters (usually up to 255 characters).
- **Boolean**. Used when there are only two data possibilities (yes/no, true/false, 0/1, red/yellow).

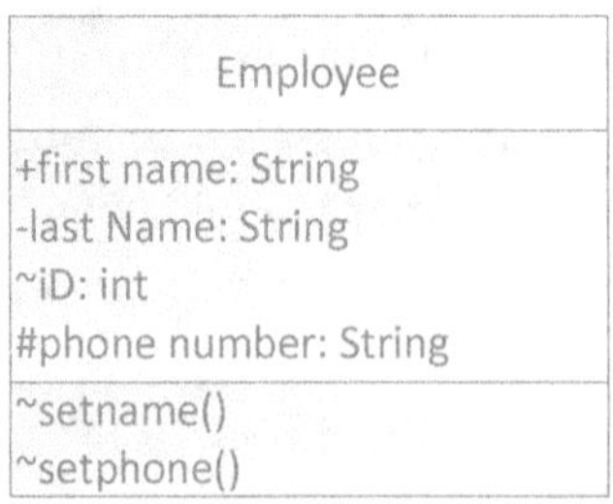

I want you to note two things in the employee example: (1) the phone number is a string, *not* an integer, because some phone numbers globally start with 0, and (2) as mentioned, some systems omit this if the zero is on the left side. Feel free to try both.

Possible Operations

The parentheses () in the operations partition will be expanded later with other values and variables from the development team. It's common practice to leave them blank as in the employee example.

The operations are the capabilities of the class to change the defined attributes. Think of it as the boundaries of control. For example, you can change and control your name and phone number, but you cannot change your height. You can also select the name of your children (child class) or choose your car (another class). An administrator can set your password; this is another example of a class impacting another class. Defining operation is the control within this class or by this class impacting other classes.

Note: Both operations and attributes start with a lowercase letter.

Relationships in the Class Diagram

Classes are interconnected with each other in specific ways. There are many different types of connections. Following are some of the most common ones used.

Association: Association is a broad term encompassing just about any logical connection or relationship between classes. Consider this connection as the fundamental connection. An example is a block and a wall linked together. But the association connection does not show why they are connected. (You can write on the line to explain.)

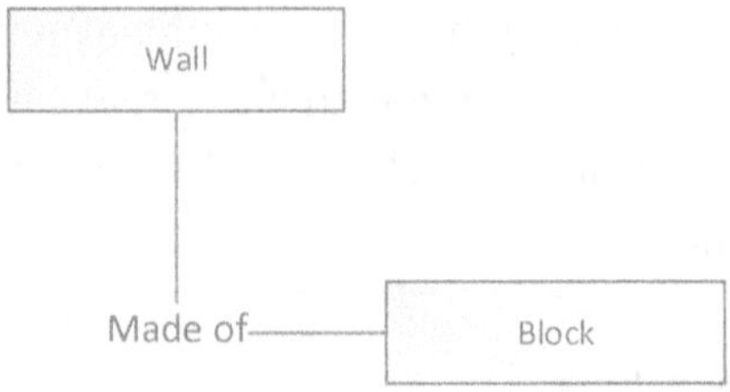

Directed association: The directed association is represented by a line with an arrowhead and refers to a directional relationship. The arrowhead represents a container–contained directional flow. This is to avoid illogical situations in developing the code.

For example, you can build a wall using multiple blocks, but you can't build a block using multiple walls. This flow control mechanism is typically used to allow flow in only one direction.

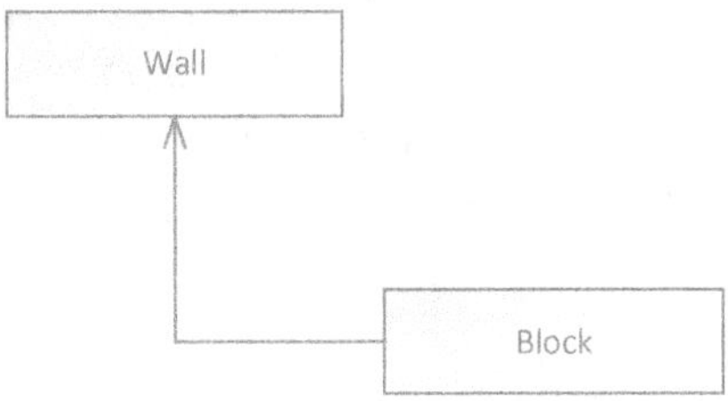

Reflexive association: Reflexive association occurs when a class may have multiple responsibilities or functions. For example, a customer list in a database may be potential customers, billing targets, upselling lists, and so on. Or a user might be an administrator and a customer simultaneously. But because of the confusing nature of this association, it's not frequently used.

Multiplicity: The number of elements of one class in relation to another class is shown through multiplicity, which is an active logical association. For example, a car can have multiple doors (one side of the connection, while one car can have two or four doors (the other side of the connection). The range or the exact numbers of the elements is shown next to the class. The options for that are:

- 0..1 zero to one (none or one)
- N specific number
- 0..* zero to many (a range from none to N)
- 1..* one to many (a range from one to N)
- A...B specific range (a defined range)

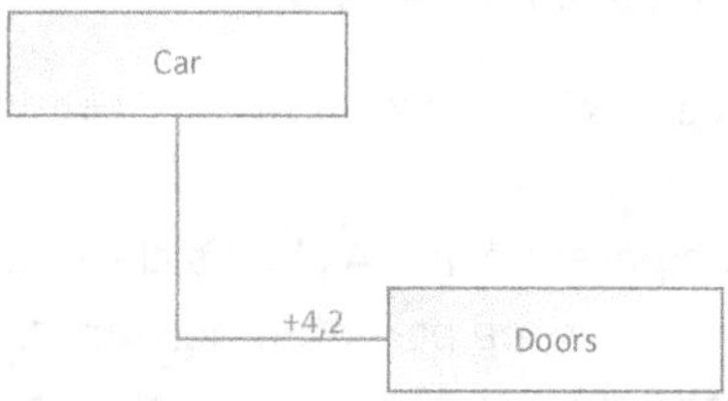

Aggregation: Aggregation refers to creating a specific class because of one class being aggregated or built as a collection. For example, there is a class "customer list" comprising one or more customers. The relation between contained class and container is weak in aggregation. In this example, the customer will remain there even when the customer list is removed. Aggregation is displayed by drawing a line from the class to the aggregated class with a diamond shape on the aggregated class's side.

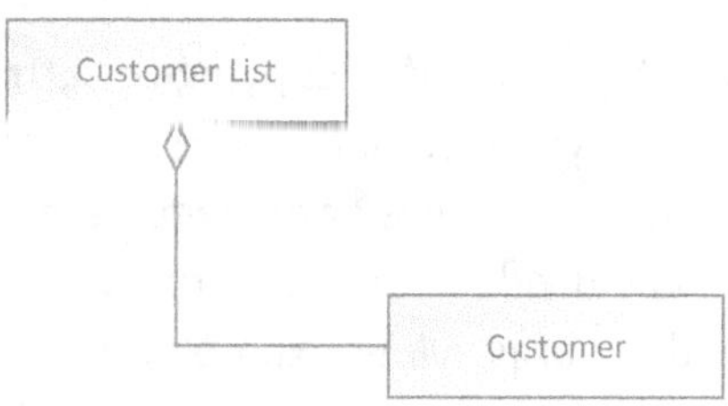

Composition: The composition and aggregation relationship is very similar, with a single difference in the relationship between contained and container classes being strongly dependent.

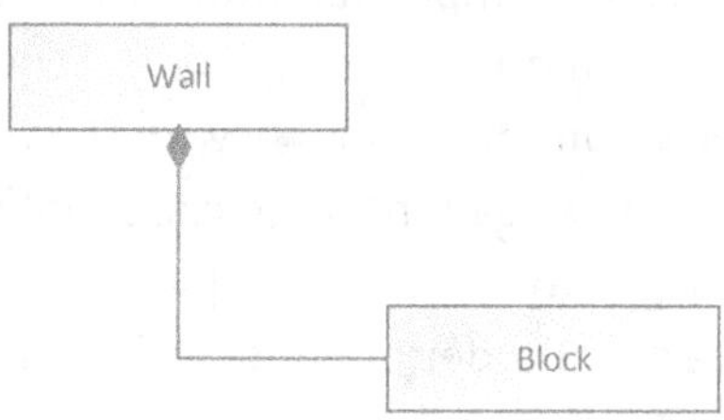

The contained class will be eliminated when the container class is destroyed. For example, the building blocks will also cease to exist once the wall is destroyed. Another example is a hotel and a lobby. The lobby could not exist without the hotel. If you remove the hotel, you automatically remove the lobby as well.

The composition is displayed through a directional line connecting the two classes and a filled diamond shape on the side that connects to the container class.

Inheritance/generalization: An inheritance or generalization shows a relationship in which one associated class is a child class while the other is the parent class. A child's class consists of the same functionalities as the parent. Inheritance is shown through a solid line from the child class to the parent class with an unfilled arrowhead.

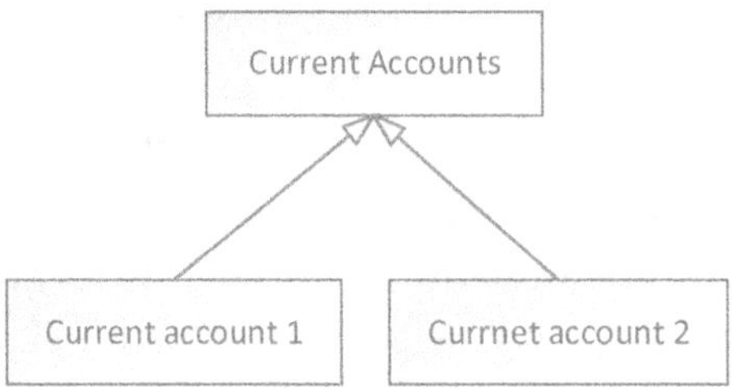

This means that instead of copying the attributes and operations across classes, you just make them inherit the attributes from the parent superclass for easier management and updating later. You can still add individual attributes to each child or the subclass. As mentioned in our previous example, the children will have the same capabilities as the father (common ones like name or age), but they also might have something to identify them that he doesn't have.

Realization/implementation: A realization relationship occurs when the functionality's implementation is defined in one class by another class. In other words, how to acquire the operations of that class. Realization can be shown with the help of a broken line having an unfilled arrowhead from the class that defines the class's functionality to the class that implements the function—for example, a client ordering supplies from a supplier or a coffee request in a coffee shop. This means the request is moved to the supplier to be able to perform and execute the action; otherwise, nothing will happen.

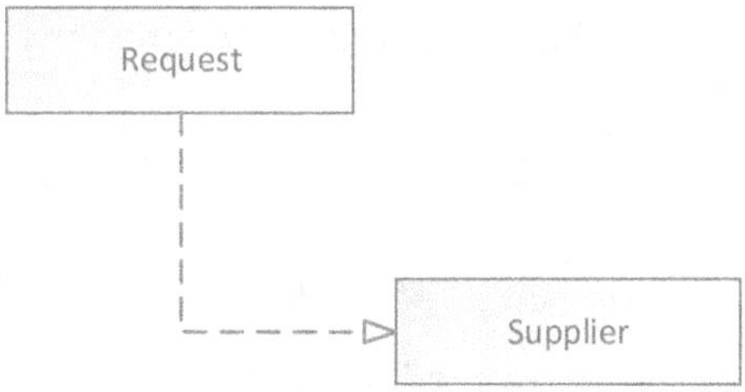

Class Diagram Example

The whole class diagram represents a layer of the system. One system could have many classes. In the following example, I will try to explain part of the online book shopping experience. Start the diagram by giving the class a name and defining its attributes. Like our general example, define the names of the major parts of your system. There is no right or wrong.

1. You have two master classes: the catalog and the users. The book's class is under the catalog as a child (there are other classes that should be in the diagram but are not shown, like audiobooks, magazines, and so on).
2. The users have two types: admins and customers. Customers can create a shopping cart and a favorites list.
3. The limitation is that a shopping cart and a favorites list can be only related to one customer (denoted by the 1).
4. One customer can have zero or one shopping cart (a customer can register but not buy anything).
5. A customer can have zero or many favorites lists.
6. The relationship between the favorites and the shopping cart is a composition because they can't exist without a customer.
7. On the other hand, there is a relation between the favorites and the books as an aggregate.
8. Next, fill out all attributes of each class.

If you notice, these are usually extracted directly from the business requirements. Because this is what usually happens—you take the customer's requirements and highlight the classes, what they should include, and how they are related.

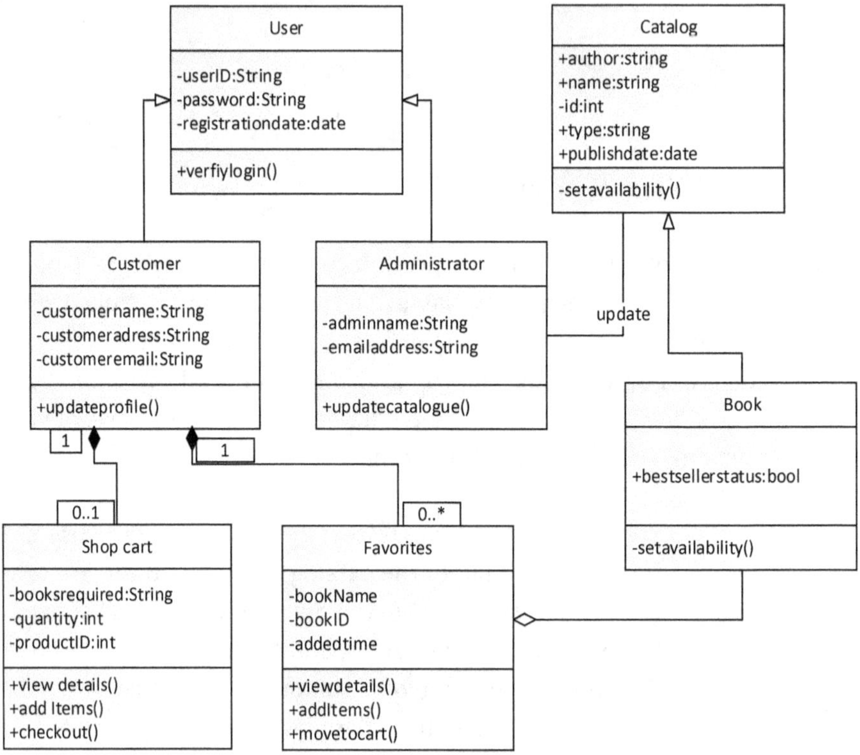

Figure 38 Class diagram example

Deployment Diagram

The deployment diagram falls into the category of a structural diagram. "The deployment diagrams" are used to provide a display of the implementation architecture of the system. It consists of the hardware implementation environment, software implementation environment, and middleware that connects both of the environments. They are used to provide a visual representation of the software and the physical hardware of a system. Compared with the other diagrams, they also assist in modeling the hardware topology instead of just outlining the logical components of a system. They greatly help in understanding the physical hardware required for executing a software system.

The deployment diagram acts as a medium to convert the architecture from the design phase into physical system architecture. This conversion will help in the real-time execution of the system and help in structuring how the software will provide placement across the physical nodes.

Why Do You Need a Deployment Diagram?

The deployment diagram is used for understanding and assisting in the deployment of a system. It explains the hardware components on which the software components are executed. That is why the deployment diagrams and component diagrams are closely related. The deployment diagram describes how the components of a component diagram are deployed in hardware. They are also helpful for the following reasons:

- Deployment diagrams help the developers focus on the hardware and software components simultaneously, unlike most diagrams that only focus on software components.
- System engineers utilize deployment diagrams to understand and focus on the hardware topology.
- Deployment diagrams are necessary to understand the run time processing that is done by nodes.
- Deployment diagrams help in understanding existing systems' requirements to integrate with recently added systems.
- Deployment diagrams play a crucial role in documenting the deployment of nodes and software components.

Pros and Cons of the Deployment Diagram

- **Pros**
    - They increase the chance of successful delivery because all the required hardware and software information becomes clear and visible.
    - They are extremely useful for systems deployed on multiple machines.

    - Deployment models are also useful in embedded systems to explain how the software and hardware components work in harmony.
- **Cons**
    - Some operational knowledge is required to develop them correctly.
    - Developing them adds to the cost of the software application.

Parts of a Deployment Diagram

There are some specific notations and elements that you need to understand to draw deployment diagrams; these are:

- Node
- Artifacts
- Devices
- Deployment specifications

Node: What is the difference between a node and a device? The difference is minimal. But it's up to you to define which is which. For example:

- You could use the word *node* for everything and not use *device* (or vice versa).
- You can use the word *node* for the workstation and *devices* for servers.
- You can use *node* for anything that will run code and *devices* for dummy terminals.

It's up to you to define the profile that describes them.

Attributes: Both *node* and *devices* should have attributes that explain that box. Under *attributes*, you list things like:

- JavaServer: server
- MySQL: DB
- Version: 8.0

You can write its name instead of the generic word *server*. Also, you can include whatever information you think is needed under the attribute.

Deployment specification: The environment required for running software is represented by a node with <<deployment specification>> stereotype.

For instance, a Java virtual machine is used for executing Java applications and is the execution environment for them. Think of it as the prerequisites or the requirements to deploy the software.

One or more deployment specifications can be in one device node.

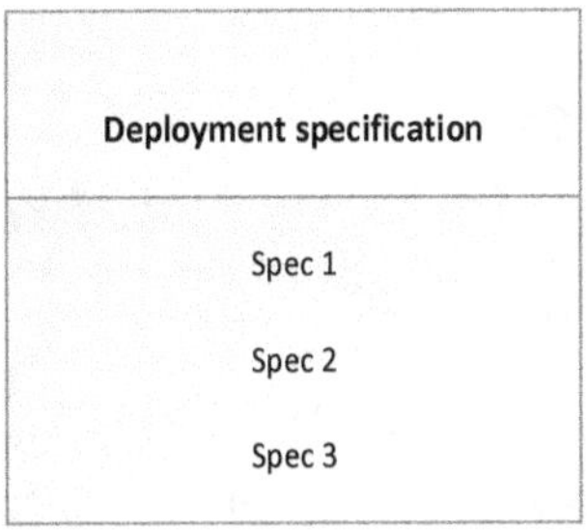

Communication association: You use the communication association to show a communication medium between two nodes. A single solid line is connected to a node on each side. You can name the protocol, such as TCP/IP, on the communication link.

Example of a Deployment Diagram

This is the deployment diagram of a bookstore: four nodes, which are named a web server, a middle server, a security server, and a database server. Customers are expected to connect over the web, though I omitted this part since there is no code or running code on the clients; it's also common to include it. It's also common to use the following shapes though it's not a standard.

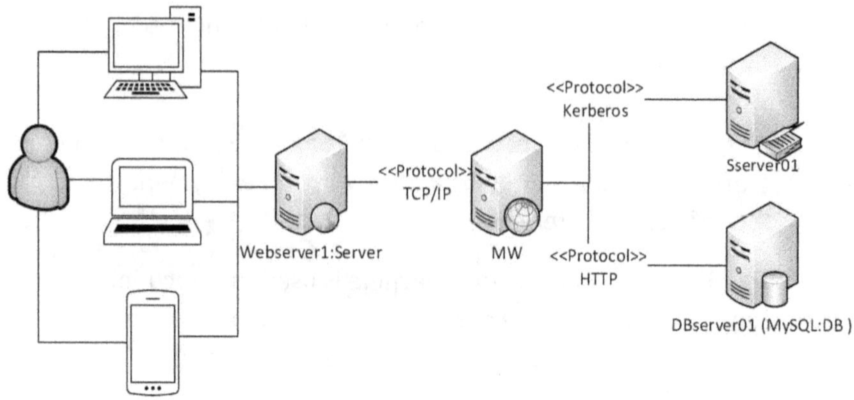

Figure 39 Deployment diagram

Behavioral Diagrams

You will need to pick at least one from the behavioral group.

Use Case Diagram

Use case diagrams belong to behavioral diagrams. A use case diagram describes/shows the relation between the actors/users and the system. There won't be a specified order in a use case diagram; the steps to reach the goal cannot be seen in these diagrams. A use case diagram is quite simple and can be easily created. It consists of a few shapes and relations. A use case is a high-level description of the requirements; each use case is a stand-alone activity.

Why Do You Need a Use Case Diagram?

The use case diagram in the system software documentation helps the developer better understand the system and user interaction. It displays system requirements in an easy-to-understand manner. Moreover, use cases help create the test cases later used by the software quality testing (SQT) team. The use case diagram is like the blueprints of software. It will show the major outer functionalities and not include the instances. It shows the dynamic behavior that is present in the system software. The actor is the person that uses the system. Like the system's blueprint, it needs to be as simple as possible. The diagrams help to identify the functions without digging deeper into the system.

Pros and Cons of the Use Case Diagram

Pros:

- It's easy to create a use case diagram.
- A nontechnical person (client) can understand them.
- It depicts the major functionalities of the system.
- It shows the relationship between different functionalities.
- It is easy to create prototypes (mockups) using use cases.

Cons:

- Drawing a use case is time-consuming due to the work of preparing the use cases and the stories.
- It just shows the functionalities and not the instances of the system.
- It does not show the order of activities.

Parts of the Use Case Diagram

The parts of the use case diagram are:

- System boundary
- Actors
- Use case
- Communication link

System boundary: The system's boundary is made up of a rectangle. The actors stay *outside* the boundary of the system. The rectangle represents the limits of the system. It's used to define system parts and outside actors.

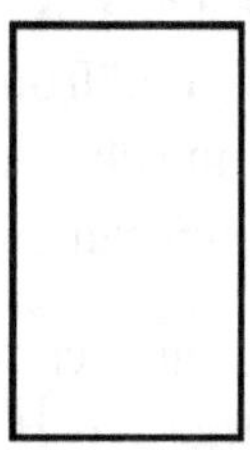

Actors: Actors in a use case diagram represent the users. An actor can be anyone from the person using the software (user or admin) to an external device or organization. The actor's role is to start the system; they need to provide some input to the system to start working. However, there will be some actors who will expect output from the system. The actor is a human doodle that interacts with the system. An actor is a group of similar users or organizations. It's not one specific person; it's an entire group of similar requirements and needs from the application. It's a straightforward drawing of a human. Based on the tool you will use, the shape will change.

Actors could be primary or secondary. The primary actors are the ones initiating the action, and the secondary ones are the ones reacting to that action.

In the online bookstore example, the primary actor is the customer opening the website. The secondary actor is the organization reacting and displaying the products available for purchase.

Placing the primary on one side and the secondary on the opposite side is possible, but there is no rule for that.

Use case: The oval shape represents the use case. Every actor/user should be linked with a use case. Some other use cases are considered internal to the system and are not linked to actors but rather to different use cases. A use case is a task the system should accomplish. These are defined from the user's point of view, not the developer's side. Something like "login" is considered one use case. Display products are considered another use case, and so on.

Note: Use cases are dynamic (actions) and start with a verb, such as login, display products, add to cart, add to favorites, and so on.

Each use case is considered a process that can be broken down further based on complexity. If the team is practicing Agile, break them down until you reach the user stories.

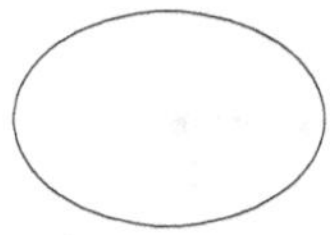

By using the mentioned components, a simple use case will look like this:

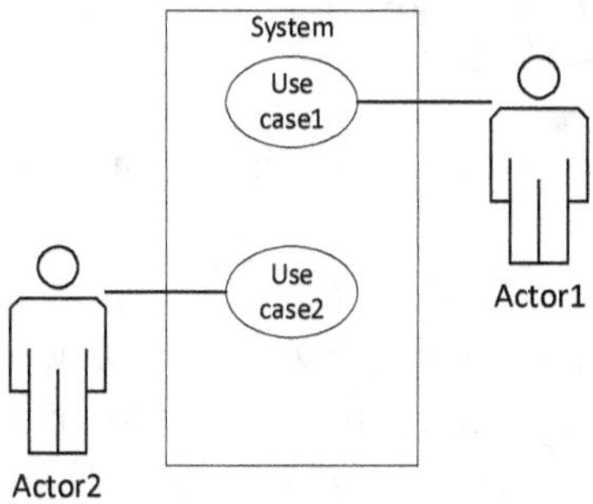

In the image, the two actors are linked with two different use cases.

Relationships in Use Cases

There are four types of relationships in the use case:

- Association
- Include
- Extend
- Generalization

Association: The communication link between the actors and the use cases present outside the system boundary. It is a link with a straight solid line.

Include: The "<<include>>" tag is used above the communication line in a use case diagram. The <<include>> relationship is present among different use cases. For example, the *login* use case must have a *validate password* use case. This means triggering the login will activate the check password use case as well. To show the *include* relationship, use a dashed line with an arrow pointing to the included use case.

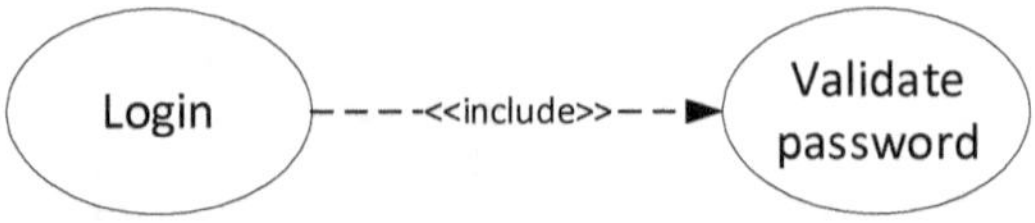

Sometimes it's called a use-use case. The base use case triggers it under all conditions. Its purpose is to simplify the base use case, make it smaller, and allow the use of a specific function across multiple use cases.

Extend: The "<<extend>>" tag is used above the communication line in a use case diagram. The *extend* relationship is used when a use case will sometimes happen only when a specific condition is met. For example, the *display wrong password* error will not happen to every user every time, so it's considered an *extend* use case. In other words, the extend tag adds specialized behavior or actions to a base use case, like a prerequisite checker or registration form for the first time.

Generalization: In this special relationship, two use cases take the input from one use case acting as a parent to a child. There could be two cases for the same action, like payment using PayPal or a credit card. The payment itself is the same, but its implementation is different. Similarly, the customer could place the order to pick up in the store or ship to an address.

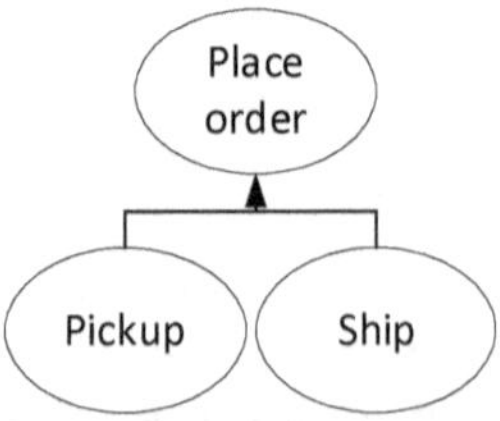

Use cases are mainly linked with the system's functionality or the software. It is highly significant that the relationship between different use cases is appropriately mentioned.

Use Cases Practices

These common practices are not a requirement, but each of the use cases needs to have the following:

- **Meta** (date created, update, by who, case name, and so on).
- **The actor** (agent).
- **Description**.
- **Business rules** should be included, if any.
- **Assumptions**, if any.
- **Preconditions** are the conditions that must be met before the use case can perform as needed.
- **Postconditions** are the conditions that happen after the use case is performed.
- **The steps**: from the precondition to the postcondition.
- **Exceptions**: why this case might not work, and how to get around that.
- **Negative case**: You could create a negative case for each of the preconditions and the steps. What if the user did something else in this step? This is useful, especially in security.
- **Glossary**: To avoid conflict, always create a definition and abbreviation table representing the meaning to the readers. This is one of the ways to reduce conflict from misunderstanding. Also, use clear, simple language.

Use Case and User Stories

Applying use cases and user stories is now quite common, especially with Agile practices. It's getting more and more focus. Use cases are similar to user stories in Agile.

User stories are simple items. For example, you should fill in the blanks of:

As a ... I want ... so that I can ...

It should not be complicated or even longer than one sentence. It should be as simple as:

As a *data entry employee,* ***I want*** *the text to automatically move to the next box* ***so that I can*** *type continuously without using the mouse to click on the text field.*

Use Case Example

Now let's take the online store as an example.

The customer in our example will try to log in (association relations), and he will get access, *or* if they've used the wrong password, they will get the incorrect password and display an error use case.

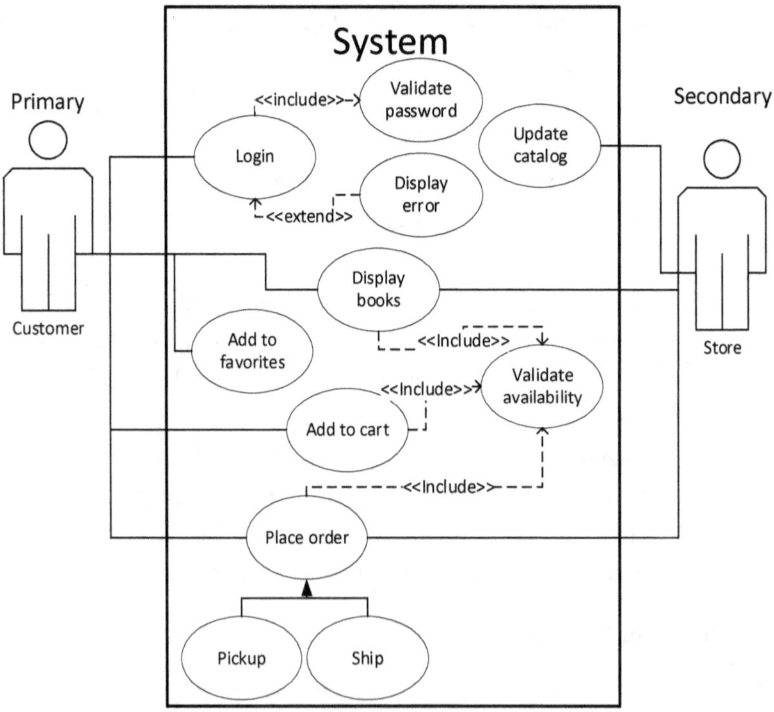

Figure 40 Use case example

Once the customer logs in, they can display the book listing. Still, before that, the availability is updated to show what's available and what's out of stock (the validate use case is on include relation).

Then the customer could add a book they like to their favorites, even if it's out of stock. Still, they can only add an available book to the cart, so a revalidation using the same validate use case is initiated to ensure that there is still stock available since they got the first display screen.

Once they add it to the cart, they can close the page or place the order. Before placing the order, the system needs to revalidate the availability. Then the customer can either request a pickup point or ship-to address.

Sequence Diagram

Sequence diagrams are used to show the sequence of interactions between the user/actor and the system. Unlike the use case diagram, sequence diagrams show the details of the operations or processes that are carried out. These diagrams show the timely order of interactions and the messages that are being sent to carry out the operation. Sequence diagrams and communication diagrams acts as alternatives, both explain almost the same thing; however, the sequence diagram is more popular.

A sequence diagram is an interaction diagram. It is one of the major and essential diagrams of software documentation. It allows the SME to understand the system requirements and the order the user is going to interact with the system. In other words, it shows the sequence of events in a particular use case and how it will flow.

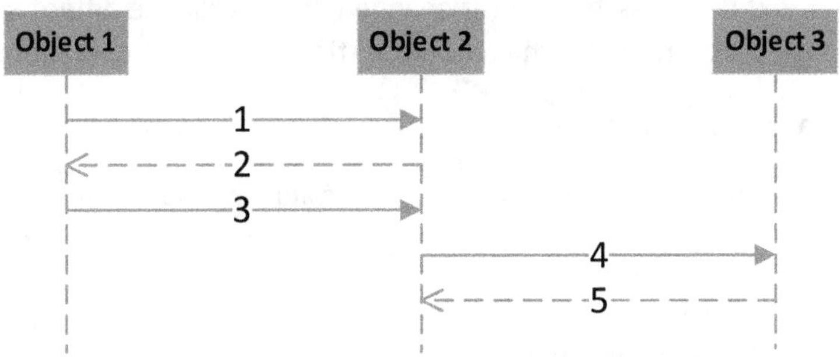

Why Do You Need a Sequence Diagram?

The best part of this diagram is that it shows the message and time when the system interacts. Sequence diagrams show the overall system design and are relatively easy to understand. The sequence diagram starts from the top and continues descending as the messages are exchanged. It represents the logic behind the functions or operations. It shows the commands and messages that take place between different components of a software system. To avoid confusion, the term *object* is not the same *object* as in the object diagram. It's the steps the user or a customer goes through to get the service. It's the large building blocks.

Pros and Cons of a Sequence Diagram

Pros:

- The real-life application can be explored with the help of sequence diagrams.
- A client from a nontechnical background can easily understand sequence diagrams.
- It is easy to maintain.
- It shows a message flow between different objects
- It identifies additional objects that were missing in the class diagram.

Cons:

- It is used to show a single stream (use case).
- These diagrams become complex if there are too many lifelines.
- If the message order is changed, it can produce different results.
- It doesn't show the amount of time between interactions.

Parts of a Sequence Diagram

A sequence diagram consists of the following major components:

- Actors
- Lifeline
- Message arrows
- Activation bars
- Comments

Actors: Actors are the entities that interact with the system by exchanging data. An actor can be any user or external hardware interacting with the system. The term *actor* is not specific to any physical entity, and it could be software or another system. The actor is represented similarly to other diagrams as a stick figure or a person's outline.

Lifeline: The lifeline shows a separate contributor in an interaction. A rectangle followed by dotted lines represents the objects.

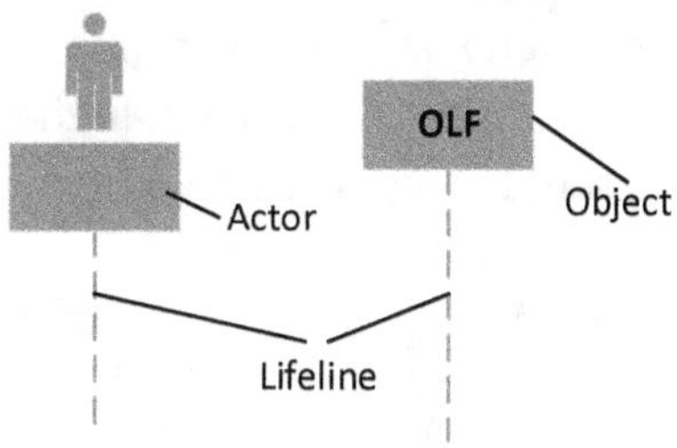

This lifeline could be for an actor, object, or even class. The sequence diagram usually gets complicated based on what you are trying to achieve, but always remember that moving down the lifeline means more time is passing.

Message arrows: Message arrows are the communication lines between different lifelines. The message shows the operation's invocation in a sequence diagram. Various messages are represented in a particular manner based on their function. The messages follow a particular format. Though this is not mandatory, it should be like "Attr=messname(arg1:class): return type" at this high level. It's also OK to write a description.

Call message: A simple call message is represented by an arrow pointing to another lifeline's activation bar. The message can be any command that an actor sends.

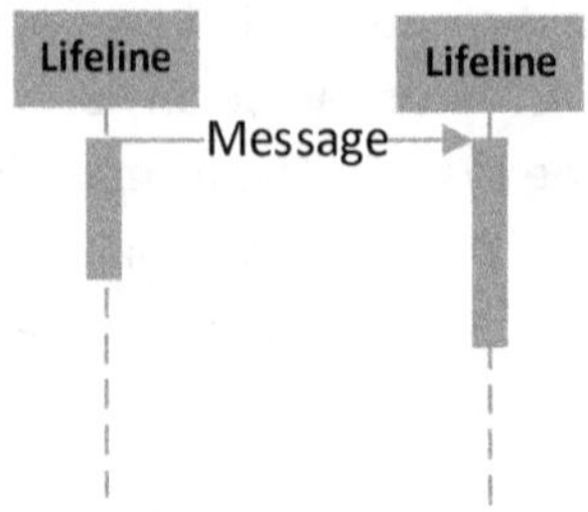

Return message: A return message is a particular message that is sent back to the caller. For example, suppose you try to log into a system and enter the wrong password. In that case, a return message will be sent to the caller: "Wrong password. Try again."

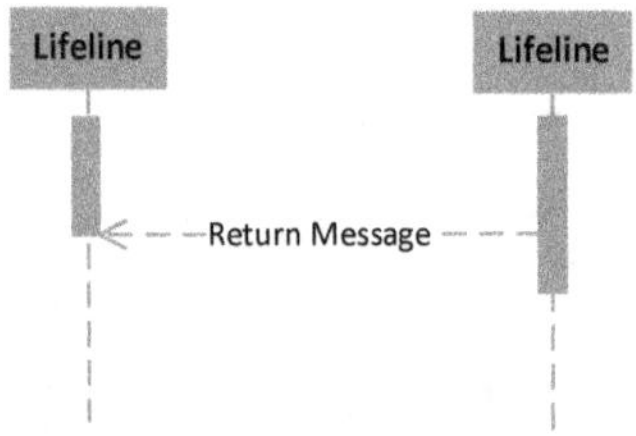

Self-message: This represents the message invocation in the same lifeline. This means the message will loop back to the sender. This happens in errors. It shows as a returning arrow (if two objects inside the class are talking to each other, and you were using classes in the timeline, not objects).

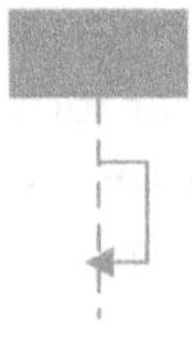

Alternative frames: Alternative frames are two choices between two message sequences (like yes/no or valid and invalid).

They will look like a framed box on top of the lifelines and messages. The top half represents the condition, and the lower half represents anything else (error).

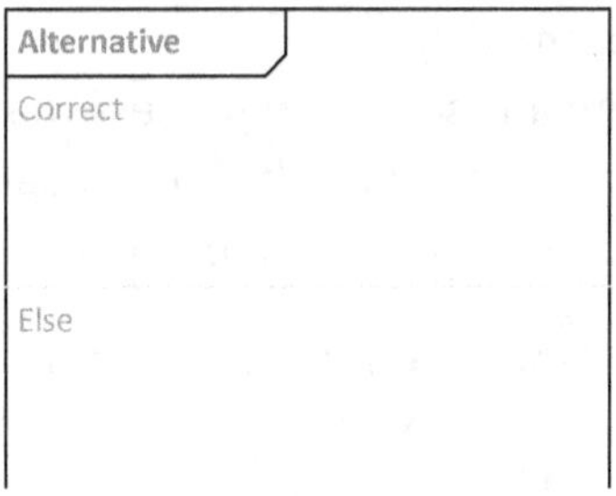

Activation bars: A thin rectangle represents activation bars; it shows the time during which an element's operation is being performed. After mapping the messages between objects, activation bars are added to understand the duration it takes for an object to finish the required process. The bar starts with the first transaction and ends with the last transaction. This thin rectangle is present between the dotted lines of the lifeline and is lined up with the initiation and completion times.

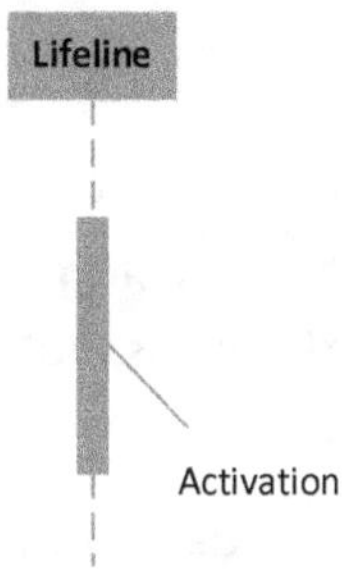

The actors don't need an activation box. After all, they are simply activated all the time because they are the ones initiating the interaction.

Comments: In a sequence diagram, with the help of comments or notes, you can attach remarks to different elements.

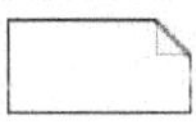

Example of a Sequence Diagram

So, the first step is to list the objects. In our example of a bookstore website, we have four main objects that the customer needs to get the desired results.

- The website (UI)
- The company server (to process the requests)
- The security database (to validate and store identity)
- The product database (the core of the website)

Our only actor is the customer. So, we draw the objects and their lifeline:

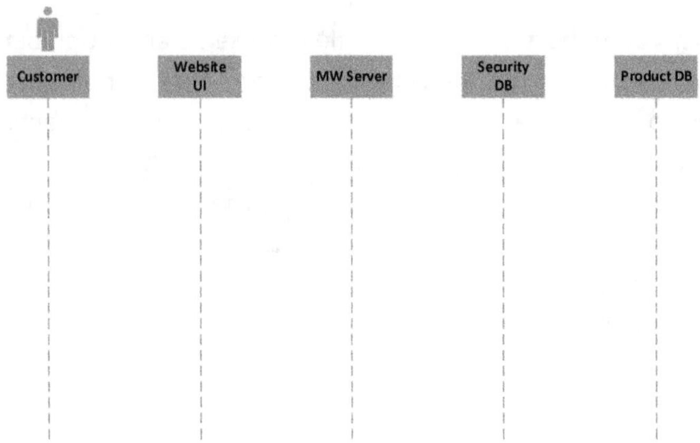

Now list the steps the actor (customer) needs to buy the required books. I am simplifying the steps, but you can go deep. So, the steps we need to be listed are:

- The customer opens a website.
- The website prepares a response.
- The customer likes something and tries to log in.

These simple steps must be translated into messages and returned messages and added to the diagram.

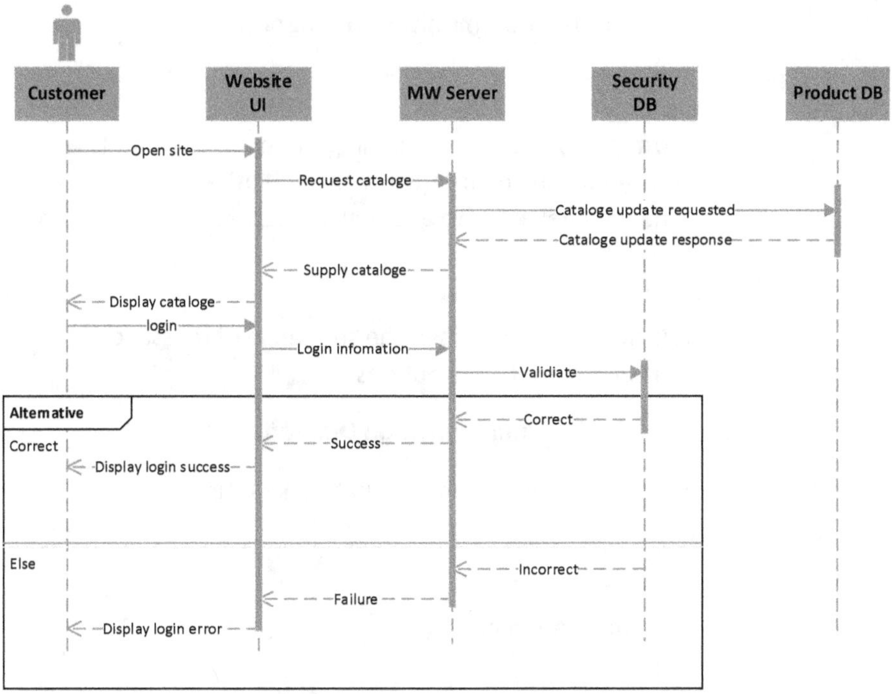

Figure 41 Example of a sequence diagram

Communication Diagram

A communication diagram, also called a *collaboration diagram*, is a diagram that shows the interactions between an object and its associated parts. It also shows the relationships between objects.

Why Do You Need a Communication Diagram?

It is known that the communication diagram and the sequence diagram are similar. Both are equivalent in terms of presenting the same information. Communication diagrams arrange elements that are in tune with space, while sequence diagrams arrange elements in tune with time. Despite being less common than sequence diagrams, communication diagrams still have their uses. Communication diagrams help visualize the relationship between different objects when asked to perform a particular task. Also, they are a great help in determining the accuracy of the static model (class diagram).

Pros and Cons of the Communication Diagram

Pros:

- It offers a better understanding of how components communicate and interact with each other.
- It has the flexibility to add new objects in two dimensions.

Cons:

- It is more difficult to see the sequence of messages.
- It has fewer notation options.

Components of the Communication Diagram

This diagram has several elements that make it up:

- Actor/user
- Use case
- Communication link
- Connector symbol
- line

Actor: The actor in a communication diagram represents the user. This could be a customer or an employee. The actor's role is to start the system. So, the process will begin by giving some input to the system. The actor is represented similarly to other diagrams as a stick figure or a person's outline.

Use case: Use cases are represented by an oval or square shape with text included. Serving as a system function, each transition leads from one use case to the next, continuing until it reaches the end of the system process. This could be a class or an object as well.

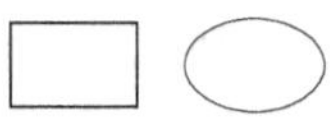

Communication link: The link serves as the bind that connects the actor and the different use cases in the diagram. It is a straight line.

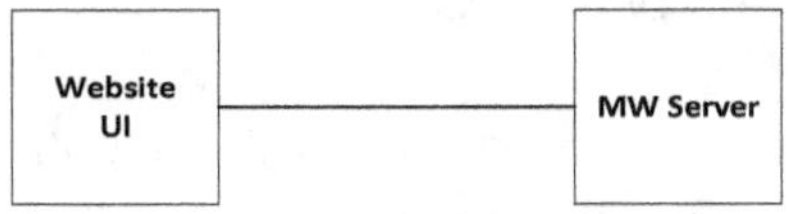

Message symbol: The connector symbol is a straight line with an arrow attached. In some cases, it can be curved as well. It is part of the transition process, which links with each use case.

The messages flow only one way. They do not go back and forth about the details of interactions; they indicate only the primary interactions between objects. You trace these messages using the numbering in front of them. For example, a message starts with 1; if it hits another object, it becomes 1.1 (not 2). This will allow you to trace each unique message to its source.

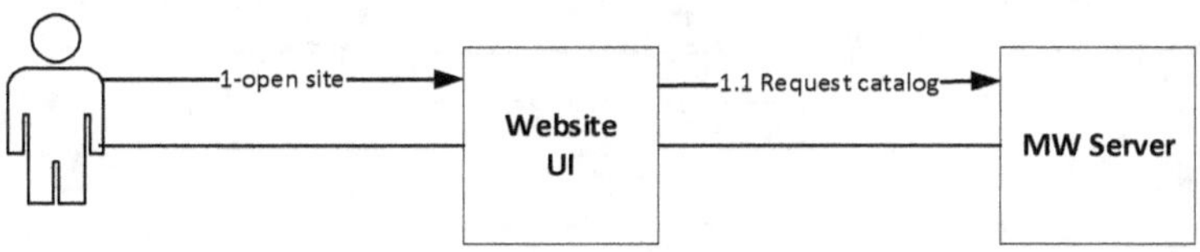

You only need to figure out how many messages there are per track. For example, if one message hits 20 different classes, you might need three branches to give you a clear vision. This is called *creating a branch*, usually used if you have some subprocess that will generate lots of messages that will not go outside this process. In this case, create a branch just to keep things clean, but it should follow the same structure as if trying to build numbering in a Word document.

1. . Initial request
    1.1.1.. security process 1
    1.1.2.. security process 2
    1.1.3.. security process 3
    1.1.4.. security process 4
    1.1.5.. security process 5

1.2. . Inventory process

Also, if you have a message sent simultaneously to another, you still give it the same number but differentiate it with a letter. For example, it becomes 1a.0, then it hits another node and becomes 1a.1.

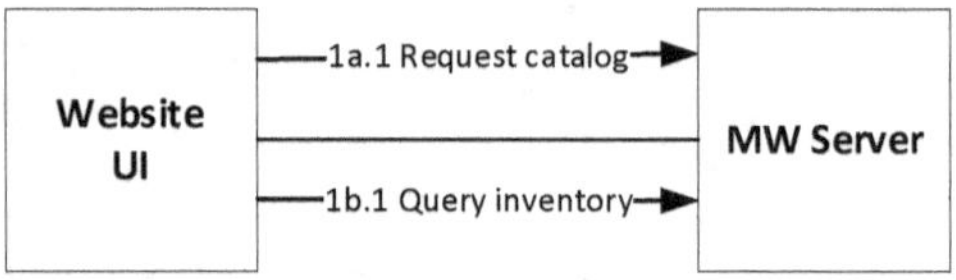

Messages with guard conditions are the messages not executed except in particular situations when a=b or A>b or something similar.

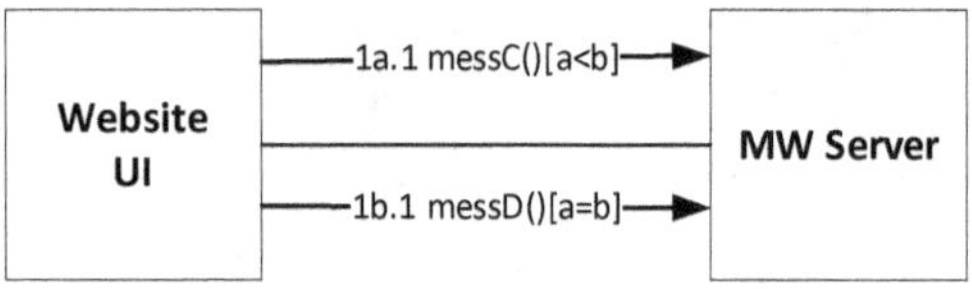

Line: The line is only seen between use cases, and it serves as a link between them. (Sometimes it's dotted, and sometimes it's solid.)

Relationships in the Communication Diagram

In the communication diagram, the main relationship would be between the use cases. The interaction between the use cases is the focus. The actor and use cases also have a relationship, but it's not the primary focus. The relationships between the different use cases impact how the diagram can be explained and perceived.

Communication Diagram Example

Let's take an example of an online bookstore where the user can search the inventory and order any book specific to this particular store. The first step is to list the objects in our example. We have four main objects the customer needs to get the desired results:

- The website (UI)
- The company server (for processing the requests)
- The security database (to validate and store identity)
- The product database (the core of the website)

Our only actor is the customer.

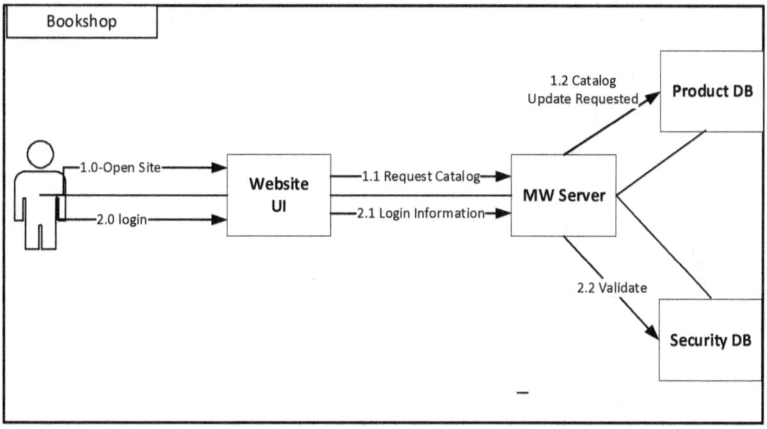

Figure 42 Communication diagram example

In the diagram, the actor initiates action by opening the website. Once this happens, the website UI requests a catalog from the main server, and the main server forwards this request to the product DB to check for a catalog update. In the next action, the user tries to log in to the website. The website UI forwards the login information to the main server, and the main server validates the information with the security DB.

Chapter 4: Model the Database with the Database Team

Database design is a domain of its own. Still, since this will significantly impact the performance and reporting capabilities of the solution, you need to understand how to design a database. This way, you can at least have the foundation to develop an application that will perform as expected. Most databases used in an application are relational databases. Some applications come with a pre-created database schema. These are usually off-the-shelf applications. You don't need to design a database in this case. All you need is to create the interface, adjust the forums by expanding the framework, and maybe create one or two additional tables to hold captured information.

The first step in building a draft model is to plan what attributes are needed. You can use any of the diagrams to determine a starting point. If you discover some attributes required to optimize the database, modify the application to include them; otherwise, it will always be blank or not populated with data. The database design is also a prototype to determine what's required, and in most cases, the database design sheds new light on requirements no one addressed before. This is why designing the database is a critical part of the application creation process; otherwise, you will have to deal with issues on the application side because you did not do the initial database design correctly.

For example, the customer address could be one field in the database. However, separating it into building, street, city, and country is best. Such separation will allow granular reporting and better table structure. Still, it will impact the forms in the application since now you need to create four fields instead of just one. You may want to let the database SME determine that. However, this decision changes the requirements, and the requirements collected could now be out of sync with reality. If no one tells the customer they must now select four fields to fill in an address, this might not be acceptable to them. So instead, find a compromise, update the wireframes, and get the approval.

Database Purpose

Now let's start from the beginning.

What Is Data?

The data is the product of business operations. This definition means you can use data around three main pillars:

- Decision-making
- Course correction
- Regulatory reasons

To reach these goals, data needs three things:

- Keep it organized to maintain it for long periods
- Secure it to ensure that no one will see something they should not.
- Generate useful information from it.

Data Keeping

Old data keeping methods still exist and are used based on the volume of data. All of these types are used to spot the need for one type and shift the model based on that.

Book Records

The first data-keeping mechanisms were the accounting and customer books as used in the past. The customer contact information is in one or two books and kept safe. And whenever needed, you can scroll/flip pages to the first letter of their name and either update their last visit or contact them. This works well if you have up to a thousand customers, maybe a few thousand even.

Spreadsheet

The spreadsheet will give you some additional benefits: searching through the data, retrieving data quickly, and determining whether any information is missing. But even spreadsheets have their limits. The challenge will be generating meaningful information, such as who last visited us/bought from us, or when updating the visit record. If you had to do it manually, it would consume lots of time.

The column in the Excel sheet is called a *field*. Each field contains a specific value, and each row contains a group of fields, usually for one customer. For example, a field may contain a name, address, or phone number. Suppose you expand this to include what they like and dislike and additional information like last visit date and allergies they have. The business will start to run into data sorting and filtering issues like in the book system. It will require some manual comparison to get to the correct data.

Relational Database

In the relational database, everything is created using tables, and the fields are broken down as much as possible to categorize the core data. Think of databases as a collection of spreadsheets, but with relationships between them and optimized data. For example, you have customer information in one table, what they like in another table, the menu in a third table, and what they ordered last time in the fourth table. Separation of data across tables will allow building a relationship between tables to determine what this customer might like in the menu and enable recommendations. The downside to this method is that modifying something is complicated and takes time, and report building is time-consuming.

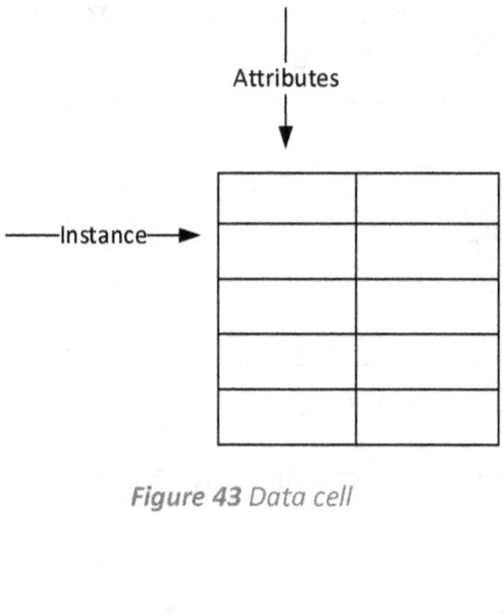

Figure 43 Data cell

The Key Concept in Databases

This complexity means you must create a key field in all the tables that refer to a specific customer. Now you have some ID that can be used across all tables and link tables together. Instead of having multiple tables for one customer, group some fields and link them using the key field. Key values are unique values that cannot be duplicated in the same table. Fields like first name and last name might be shared across customers. So, either find something unique about the customer (like a user name) or generate this field to ensure you can identify each customer.

It's possible to make a key out of anything based on the database management solution. Still, I have found it useful to add a field dedicated to the key. This key is called a *synthetic* key. It's named that because it's not part of the original data. And you use it as a reference across multiple tables to build relationships. More on that later. The key cannot be changed. This is why we never use phone numbers as keys. Unexpected changes to fixed things (like phone number) are also why many SMEs prefer synthetic keys because they are independent of business operations.

Let's look at an example to understand better how a database works.

Draft a Database Model

You have a few things in the online bookstore example that will be requesting specific attributes in the database. To define these entities, go back to class, sequence, or use case diagrams. In the example, the entities are:

- The books
- The customers

These are the initial attributes required. Additional attributes should be included based on business requirements.

For the customers, maintain the following attributes:

- First name
- Last name

- Address
- Email
- Is administrator
- UserID (synthetic key)

Users					
UserID	First name	Last name	Address	Email	Is administrator
1	Jane	Doe	NW	x@Y.com	No
2	John	Doe	ST	Z@M.Co,	No
3	John	Doe	CA	W@H.org	Yes

Table 9 *User table*

For the books, maintain the following attributes:

- Book name
- Author name
- Type
- Publishing date
- Best seller
- BOKID (synthetic key)

Books					
BOKID	Book name	Author name	Type	Publishing date	Best seller
1	Harry Potter	J.K. Rowling	Book	1997	Yes
2	Lord of the Rings	J.R.R. Tolkien	Book	1954	Yes
3	Defiance	Nick Webb	Book	2017	No

Table 10 *Books table*

After the *customer* and *books* tables, two special tables are also required (*favorites* and *cart*). Since the customer could have zero or many in each, it will be wasting database space if you keep adding fields (columns) next to the customer name with favorites or cart. Though it would function, it will cause issues after the customer base reaches a certain size, since, as mentioned, one customer could have 200, and another could have zero. Create new tables with "many to many" relationships to solve this problem. *Many to many* means keys from other tables linked. The many to many relationship links the customer table keys and book table keys in one table as rows. Sometimes, this is referred to as a bridge table. And this is considered a special table.

Favorites table	
BOKID	UserID
10	5
12	5
14	5
10	2
10	90
19	3

Table 11 Favorites table A

This table shows that customers with UserID 5 have books 10, 12, and 14 in their favorites, and customer 2 has book ID 10 in theirs. Now, the same concept applies to the cart table. Create a key for this table to identify each row as well.

Favorites table		
FavID	BOKID	UserID
1	10	5
2	12	5
3	14	5
4	10	2
5	10	90
6	19	3

Table 12 Favorites table B

These tables show that with each record, the customer clicking "add to favorite" will create a new document (row) in this table, generating a unique ID and mapping the user ID to the book ID.

These are the basic ideas you need to build a database. With all of these ideas in mind, you need to start building the actual model using an ERD diagram.

Model the Database Using ERD

The *entity-relationship diagram* (ERD) demonstrates the data schema in a database and how it connects. The ERD helps us understand the interactions between data, optimize the database storage, and tune the performance early on.

Why Do You Need an ERD?

As mentioned previously, the database is one of the significant contributors to the application's performance; if poorly designed, performance will drop significantly. Also, changing the database is quite tricky after the actual application implementation. Extending it is possible, but rearranging the data is not easy. In the field, I see many databases that had one extension after another added to the point where it takes hours to complete a simple operation or to generate a report. So, it's better to understand the customer data requirements and plan for them.

Parts of the ERD

- **Entity**: Things in the model about which you need to keep data. In the example, the *books* and the *users* (customers).
- **Attributes**: This is the information you wish to keep about the entities. They are of several types:
    - **Simple**: Single value, like ID number or serial number (cannot be separated into multivalue or multi-part).
    - **Composite**: Multivalued, having several components, like an address (Apt#, Street#, City).

  You can also have attributes either *stored* or *derived*:

    - **Stored**: Input gathered directly from the user.
    - **Derived**: Attributes that can be generated based on other information. For example, if a birth date is available, the system can quickly calculate the age.

ERD Shapes

There are two primary schools in diagramming a database and building the ERD: Chen's database notation and UML database notation. The first one focuses on understanding the difference between the shapes and diagramming a very detailed database design. The UML is quite simplistic, and it's sufficient for diagramming a database model.

	UML	Chen's
The entity		
Attributes		Attribute
Multivalued attributes	N/A	Attribute
Derived attributes	N/A	Attribute
Primary key	PK Attribute name	Attribute
Weak entity (No value can be key)	N/A	
Relationship		

Table 13 ERD shapes

Relationships (Cardinality)

One-to-one: One row of data is connected to another single table row. This is used when separating parts of the data across tables or databases. Like the user name/password relationship, you cannot have them both in one table. You must separate the tables by applying additional security to both. (Rarely used.)

One to Many (or Many to One): Customer ID relates to multiple things, such as favorite books.

Many to Many: Used to create special tables like favorites, or in complex scenarios where users will have multiple instances in rows.

These are the basics. There are many more used in different cases and different scenarios.

Applying What You Learned

Let's look at a straightforward example to demonstrate the connections between customer keys with many orders.

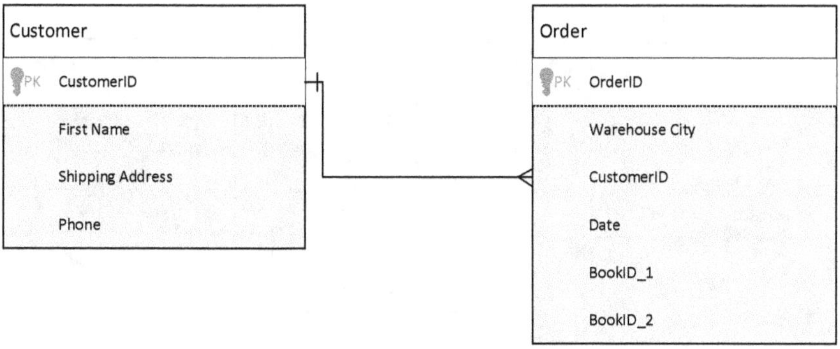

What Does This Connection Mean?

- From left to right (one to many), a single customer ID can exist many times in the orders table.
- From right to left (many to one), all orders with the same customer ID can be traced to one customer.

The linking between tables is done through keys. You might also have noticed that this will generate too many records in the order table because each customer can order only two books per order number (because the order table has only two available fields for book ID). And either the customer will have to reorder to get more books, *or* the system will generate multiple orders. You will have to create another delivery table to patch all these orders together. As mentioned, this is not the recommended way, but it's shown for the sake of demonstration. Instead, use the bridge tables.

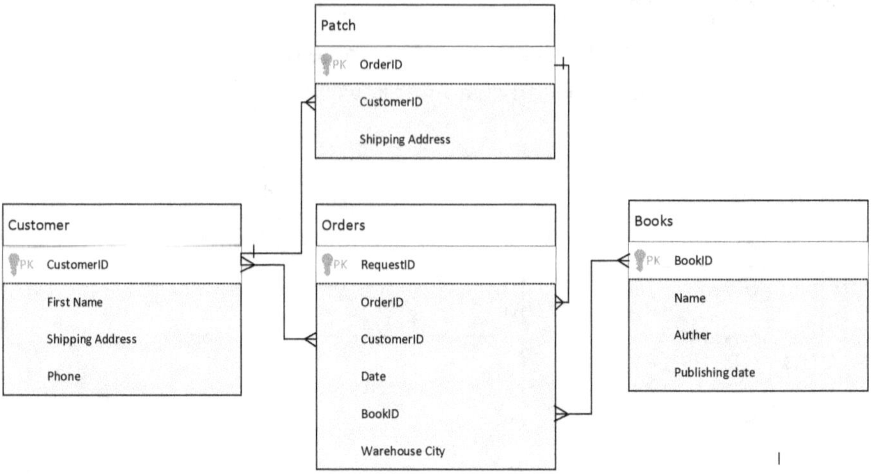

Figure 44 ERD example

This will allow each customer to generate an "orderID" per shipping address, and each order ID could include as many items as the customer wishes. I know this might sound not very easy; in reality, this is a very simplistic application. The whole objective of drawing the ERD is to understand the restrictions that exist because of how the data is stored. This will require the capture of information you never thought the application would require, such as the purchase date and time and when a customer performs this "buy operation." The application will need to generate many things, like the order number given to the customer, but the application generates many requests on the back end. Each request maps to one specific book/item that will be part of this order. As mentioned earlier, you don't have to draw a technically compliant diagram. But you need to think about this because this will save you many issues down the road.

Database and Agile

So, what about Agile? Should the databases follow the same practice? The database usually adapts to that, but the initial design must be done based on the original use cases at the beginning of the project.

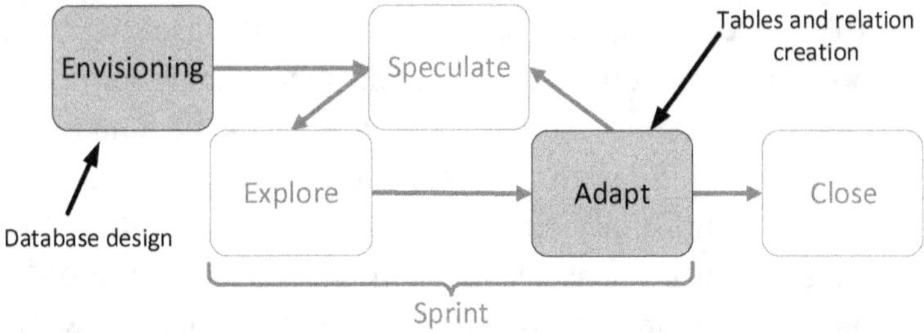

The database itself does not need to be built from the start, but you need to understand the basics of the application use cases and the data captured when creating a database. This is why it's called a *structured* database. It's structuring data in tables, rows, and columns, and building relationships between them. And changing such a structure is not easy. So, it's better to start with the absolute minimum, follow the core best practices, and extend the data by adding a field or new tables with each release. So, to avoid slipping into data duplication or allowing performance to decline, you need to be mindful of the basic database optimization rules to ensure that each release will not impact the application.

Database Optimization

Database optimization can address the database management system (DBMS) (Oracle, MS SQL, MySQL, and so on) and the database structure. An example of DBMS optimization is adjusting the memory building indexes. And this is usually part of the daily operations of a database administrator (DBA). Nowadays, all database management systems run from memory. This levels the playing field in terms of speed. Still, if you have a large database or plan to have one, it's good practice to optimize the data to improve the engine functionality and performance. It's good practice when building your database to ensure it will not require an extension (adding columns or tables) or database redesign and migration.

An alternative to structured data is *unstructured data*. In unstructured data, you store the data without knowing the relationship between the items. Think of it as a large block of text dependent on some level of AI to analyze and extract meaningful data from it.

The concern as a BA usually will be the database structure, for the previously mentioned reasons. You should know some basic rules of data optimization to understand how to build a fundamental database. This design knowledge will allow you to discover more requirements. It all comes down to the expected data size. If you have a small database, it will not matter because the DBMS engine's power and being able to load all the data in memory will make these changes minimal. Still, if you plan to have a relatively large database, consider this.

The general practice for data optimization is to reduce data duplication. It's the practice of eliminating the duplication between the rows and columns and preventing repeating data.

Not Normalized			
ID	Book Name	Type	Book
1	Harry Potter	Book	Yes
2	Lord of the Rings	Book	Yes
3	Defiance	Book	Yes
4	Defiance	Book	Yes

Table 14 Not normalized

In Table 14, you have one row that has duplicated information (ID 3 and 4 are the same), and the fields "Type" and "Book" result in the same information, but instead of a row, it's column based. So, you can optimize this by removing the duplication in data (you can remove the row or the column, based on what you think is the best fit for your situation).

Case 1		
ID	Book Name	Book
1	Harry Potter	Yes
2	Lord of the Rings	Yes
3	Defiance	Yes

Case 2		
ID	Book Name	Type
1	Harry Potter	Book
2	Lord of the Rings	Book
3	Defiance	Book

Table 15 Normalized

Next, proceed to table optimization rules. This is called *normalization* and has many rules, but the first three are the main rules

First normal form: This is easily spotted if one of the following is the case:

- Ensure that each cell has only one piece of information. Not a list like "customers like A, B, C."
- To explain the customer's desires or wants, you generate more fields by adding a number to fields like books 1 and 2. If there are numbers next to the field, this is considered bad.

You could continue with normalization forms second, third, and beyond, but this is a domain of its own, and you don't need it as a BA. I am just listing them for information purposes.

Second normal form: Any data you could extract from part of the data (one field continuously shows up with another field).

Third normal form: No data can be extracted from another field based on the general rule, like "price" and "price after discount." So, if you offer the same discount on all items, you add a field called *price after discount*. In this case, you know how much it will be because your discount is fixed. But if you offer a discount only on some items, that's OK because the rule is not a general rule.

Chapter 5: Model Report with the Data Analyst Team

The primary objective of this chapter is to define the reporting requirements of the application or the system you are trying to construct. This avoids rework and ensures correctly collected data and well-built forms/screens. The major restriction in generating the report is data. If the data is unavailable, the application must capture a good amount before generating the report. To decide if the data is enough, you need to understand the business value of this system and how it will be used in decision-making. Nowadays, most organizations have a data visualization tool, like Tableau or PowerBI. These tools connect to the data sources and generate friendly dashboards. And they allow for constructing premade reports that can be published to others. So, the first part of designing the reporting requirements is to plan how many reports the application will need.

How Many Reports Should You Plan?

The system output consists of three main types:

- *Display screens* are usually used as feedback or overview from the system, like display history, orders, or profile page.
- *Informational reports* offer background information or specific information needed.
- *Analytical reports* are usually generated by a person to solve a problem and offer recommendations like a business case.

A report could be in any medium, such as a dashboard, printed report, or display report. The medium through which the user will consume data makes little difference.

Report creation is a never-ending endeavor. Many organizations hire developers to create reports and adjust the application forms to include more fields to generate additional information. In other words, reporting requirements evolve to match the business need to increase visibility and facilitate decision-making. Think of it as a flashlight in a dark room. The business needs to adjust it occasionally to shed light on some aspects.

There are no standards regarding the reporting limits of a system. But as starting point, reports are made *per* stakeholders group, not individually. So, typically, when a group of users provides specific requirements such as shipment delivery time or warehouse stock, it's reasonable to say they might be interested in seeing such a report. A report is the fruit of the system being built and designed earlier. Go back to the stakeholder's identification matrix and expand it with one interest from that group.

Internal	Success Criteria (Primary Interest)	Reporting Requirements
Boss	Smooth delivery	Shipments per day
VP	Profitability	Sales per day
Users	Operations	Orders
The technical support team	Visibility	Incidents
Finance department (John Doe)	Customers collection	Payments

Table 16 *Stakeholder success criteria*

Based on these interests, build a nonvisual prototype from scratch with the user in a separate meeting or a workshop after the requirements gathering to ensure that the critical reporting requirements for that group are captured. Another reason for making this a separate meeting is to avoid the stakeholders focusing only on the requirements provided during the session.

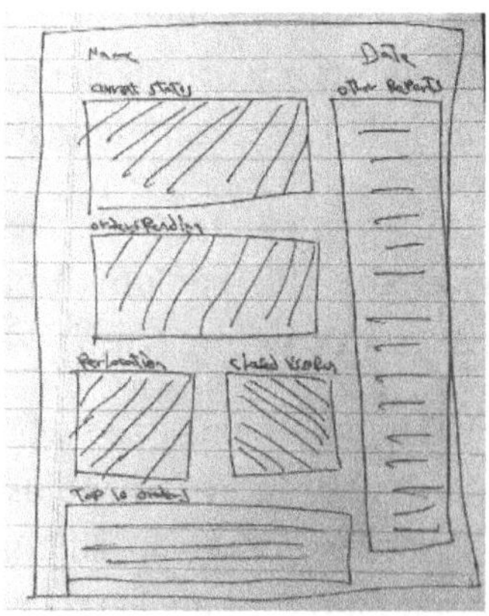

Figure 45 *A nonvisual prototype for a report*

There is a big chance you will discover additional requirements and information that need to be included in the application to generate the desired result from the system. In this case, go back to the original requirements captured earlier and expand them to include these new findings. The main issue is that the stakeholders will provide the requirements in all directions without showing a logical connection. However, it might be a valid need, but the report requirements will seem unrelated. So, typically, this is the next step in ensuring the model is correctly constructed.

The next step is optimizing the reports to tell a story and enhancing the graphics to assist decision-making. Let's start with why this is critical. It's always safer to perform actions based on false-positive responses (the prisoner's dilemma from game theory is an example). However, this is not the maximum outcome of the decision. It's always easier to say no than yes, especially if a risk is involved. So, to avoid having unfavorable responses every time, the report's story provides assistance to walk the decision-maker through the decision-making process and tell them the full story by focusing on their needs. So, you do these report enhancements to facilitate acting on the information by focusing on the flow of the report and the information contained in it.

Optimize the Reports for Decision Making

Though the process is the same across all decisions, a decision has three categories:

- Simple decision (the day-to-day work)
- Simple decisions with significant impact
- Strategic decision (requires more time to study, and typically the report is presented as a business case)

How to distinguish between the three? The day-to-day report has a low impact on the future of the organization. However, the strategic report significantly affects how the organization operates and typically has a large investment associated. Examples of such reports include mergers and acquisitions and major initiatives like restructures. Also, strategic decisions usually have an element that does not exist in simple decisions: high levels of ambiguity, competitive response, and contingency plans.

Steps for Decision-Making

Decision-making is a six-step process, each representing an opportunity to build and develop reports to assist in decision-making.

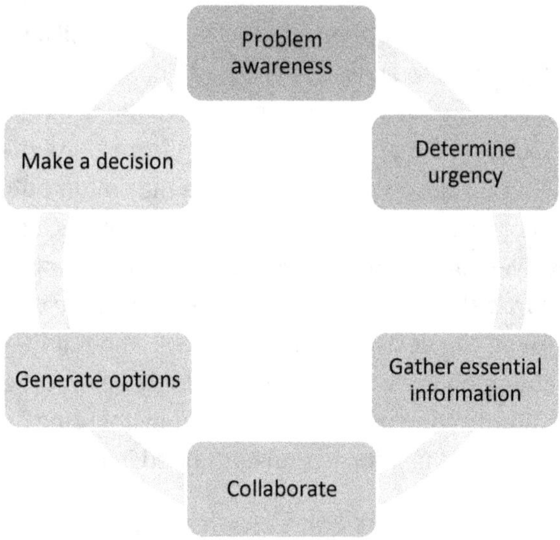

Figure 46 *Decision-making process*

Problem awareness: The first step in decision-making is understanding the business's problem; this is where key performance indicators (KPIs) come in. If the results match these KPIs, everything is fine, but if not, it's unacceptable, and a problem is defined. This could be the actual problem or only the symptom of a problem. This is why additional reporting might be needed, and requested overtime.

Determine urgency: How long is allowed for problem analysis before deciding? This is based on the impact of the problem. The more impact the problem has, the more urgent the situation will be. For example, an order delivery one-day delay will cause an issue but not as much as if the website is down. A business impact analysis study determines urgency.

Gather essential information: Drill down to understand more about the problem and determine the best course of action to solve it. This could be other reports in the system or even developing new reporting capabilities entirely. Usually, gathering enough information in this area helps if two metrics are available: *leading indicators* (the indicators present before an event happens, like a sales pipeline) and *lagging indicators* (indicators seen after an event, like sales quotas achieved). If the business measure is only lagging, it will always be reactive. But analyzing the leading indicators will present more options to solve the problem.

Collaborate: In collaboration, solicit input from the team to gather more information about the situation and present several options to solve the issue.

Generate options: Ask the following questions:

- What is the ideal situation?
- How many paths lead to this ideal situation?
- Who will be impacted by this decision?
- Can they accept the new decision, or will this generate a new problem?
- What are the constraints? (Time, money, rules, regulations, internal politics, and so on.)

Based on these questions, generate a range of options.

Make a decision: After the previous step, weigh the options and take the most likely decision prospects to succeed.

Report Parts

As mentioned earlier, if you use a visualization tool, things will be much simpler. But generally, reports should have three things:

- Text
- Graphics
- Additional information (links to other reports)

It's common to use graphics to summarize a large volume of data; it's an amazing analysis tool, but don't forget the importance of the real data tables from the report. Each report should have two versions, one graphics-based and the other text-based. Additional data will support the problem analysis. If you are using a tool, it will provide this functionality automatically. The tool will also give a drill-down function and allow the user to customize the report dashboard as they wish.

Align the Parts of the Report to the Decision-Making Process

Mapping the decision-making process to the relevant parts of the report, you should have the following:

- Problem awareness—where we have been, where we should be, and highlighting the gap.
- Determine urgency, the impact of the problem (customer morale, financial, and so on), the before and after states, and the gap.
- Gather essential information (the sub-indicators that contribute to the primary indicator).
- Collaborate (have a share by email option in the reports, for example, with the ability to ask others questions).
- Generate options: who or what will be impacted by this decision? For example, the responsible team's workload as well as the alternative team's workload, capacity, and so on.

Using these elements will help in decision-making.

Report creation doesn't stop there. Things like what graphics to use and the value of a line chart versus a histogram chart are also very important. This is an entirely different topic of data visualization. For example, the before/after states and the gap could be highlighted with one graphic for easier understanding. An excellent book on this topic is *Storytelling with Data: A Data Visualization Guide for Business Professionals* by Cole Nussbaumer Knaflic. You will also find many YouTube videos by her about the same subject. I would also recommend an infographic called "The Graphic

Continuum" from Jonathan Schwabish and Severino Ribecca. It will show you at a glance what type of graphic should be used in a specific situation.

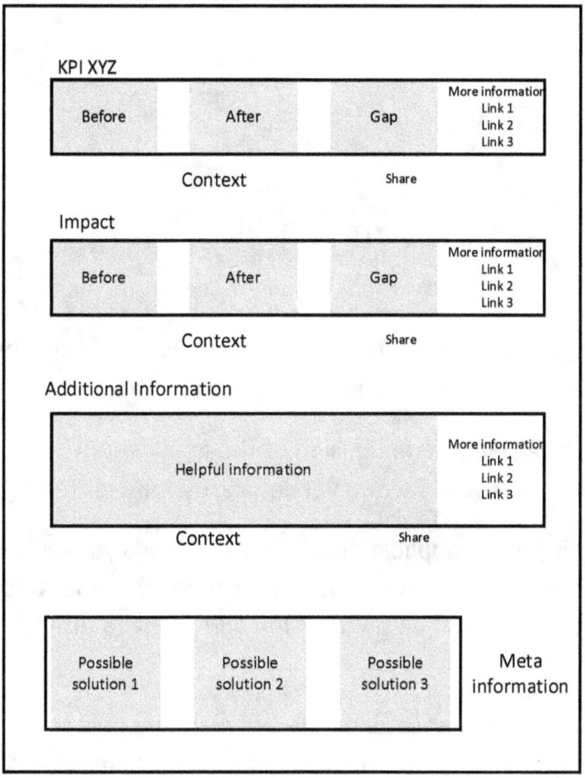

Figure 47 *Report layout*

Of course, you will still have the standard informational report, like orders of the day. Utilizing the framework mentioned, you could not merely build information but avoid an issue becoming a problem because you highlight the gap every time.

After finalizing all the data, this information will usually require one more round with the stakeholders to ensure you have all of the success criteria and KPIs from the beginning of the project. Also, include additional fields in the application to ensure the report will be generated correctly.

Before Moving On

As mentioned at the beginning of the book, you should have a valid application model at this point. You have all the parts, from the interface to the business intelligence.

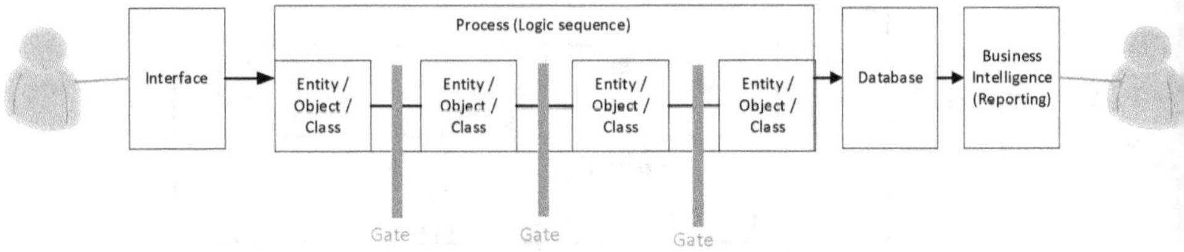

Figure 48 Application composition

Though each part of the application should impact other parts, you should go through two rounds of building the model:

- Alpha (the first vision of the application)
- Beta (the second version ready for user testing)

The bigger the application, the more rounds you will need. But in all cases, it will take several iterations to decide what to do. At this point, you should be on day nine and ready to present the findings to the team.

In the next two chapters, I discuss planning how these applications will be deployed into the production environment and relate to the requirements. Such discussions happen with the SMEs during the model-building phase. I have found this process straightforward, and it usually doesn't take that much time. But nevertheless, this discussion needs to be cleared before presenting the final results to the customer.

Chapter 6: How the Design Impacts Functionality

Technology experts are always trying to find ways around the complexity problem. The goals are to make changes smaller, easier to manipulate, and, best of all, simple to reverse. Efforts to achieve this level of complexity and agility have led to a better understanding of the need for a start-to-finish cycle of the change process that includes development, deployment, and maintenance. Those focusing on only one part will achieve 33 percent of the results. Those focusing on all three will achieve a smarter, more agile organization. A few efforts to address this are already in play, like DevOps and multiple Agile methodologies. This chapter will overview how technology enables faster, smarter change.

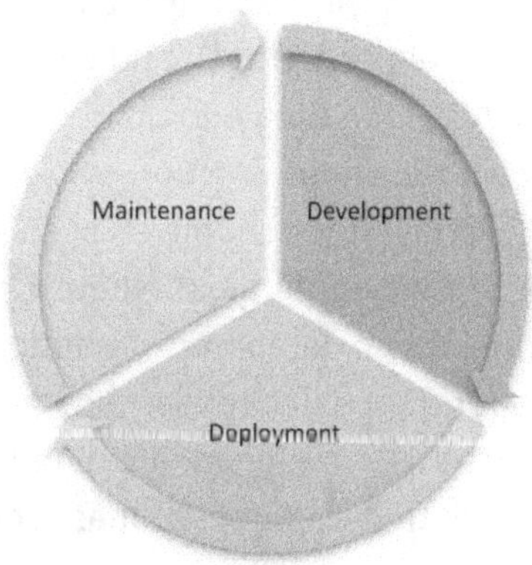

Figure 49 Relation between phases

Here's an example of how a simple setup can become complicated. Any information delay will cost money if you build a system running real-time operations like retail, hospital, or factory operations. In these instances, systems usually are built for speed. And to reach this speed, each entity or department will receive a small database for faster access. The database structure itself will be built using tables designed to reduce load times. This setup aims to maintain a database as small as possible and move elements not marked as operational into a separate database. The result is a system akin to the structure of a tree.

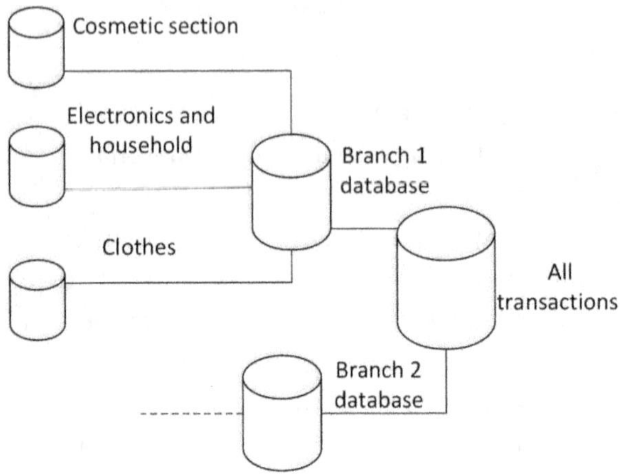

Figure 50 *Level one connection*

In a retail example, this structure takes the transactions from each department within one branch and consolidates them into a single branch database. The data end up in one database, but it is not optimized for efficient interaction by business intelligence. Things like ML and AI do not function well at this level for lack of data to build a model. Consequently, the data is transformed into another format in the branch database that holds all the data. Though some might consider the final database a data warehouse, it typically isn't. As previously mentioned, it's built for speed, and its existence seeks to ensure that the first database remains small. Since this database contains only one type of data—the transactions in this example—it's quite challenging to extract business intelligence. While generating a key report, like sales within a specific time frame, is possible, a more detailed analysis is difficult.

To make a system provide more meaningful information, start by creating data linkage from inception to after-sales support. This integration among databases will yield additional business indicators. To begin, all data from differing streams should be copied to one database. The data is prepared in another format for injection into the data warehouse database. Usually, this is the stage at which business intelligence will begin to appear. With data on one database, meaningful reports may be generated throughout a business.

This is the power of consolidation. It can generate all data for all business needs. In a fragmented state, by comparison, managers can still generate reports, but the process will take longer to generate the report and run the query across multiple databases.

The calculation for the operational database metrics is transactions per second. Still, in business intelligence systems, the metric used is query response time. In other words, the system is designed in the first few levels to quickly accept transactions to meet customer needs. The system remains optimized to generate fast decision-making reports and produce them quickly at the back end.

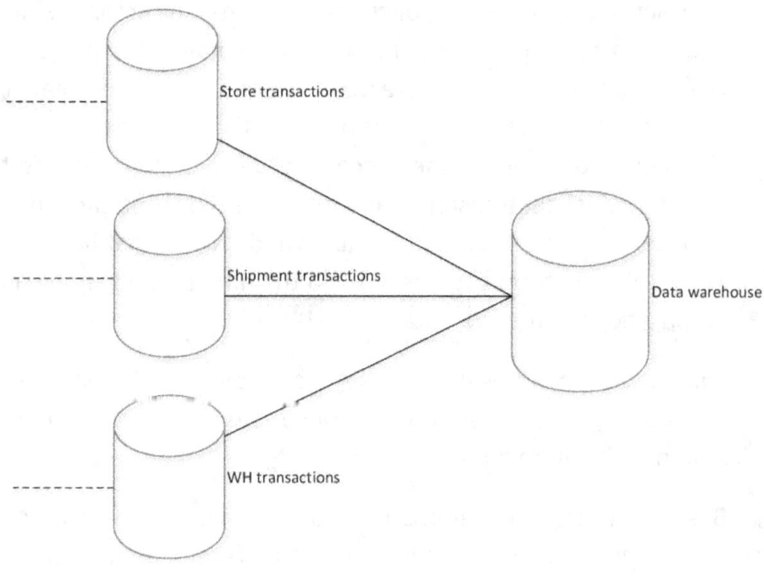

Figure 51 Level two connections

Now, let's take this up one more level.

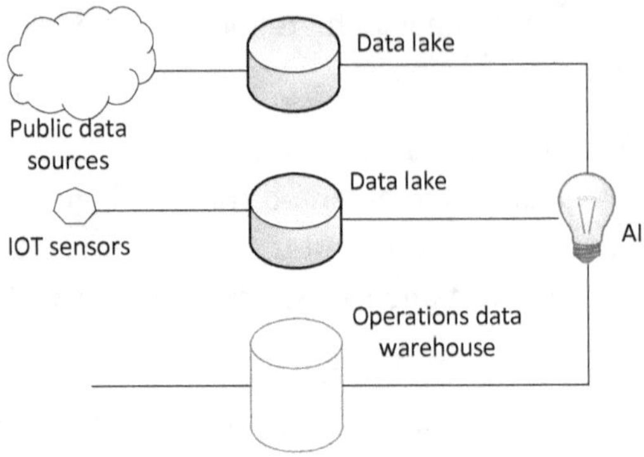

Figure 52 Advanced levels

At this level, data comparisons begin along with those of transactions. That means collecting new data on customers' written public content like reviews and Facebook comments. Analysis of all will require an AI, typically created to augment decision-making and highlight areas that need attention. This diagram is significantly abstracted to introduce the concept. Usually, it will be an additional layer to translate, transform, and integrate data. The same is true for AI. Usually, an AI system has its own data sets that have extracted data from sources to build the data training model in preparation for the live data.

This example clarifies that a system is usually built for either speed or reporting. Though you can use one system for both, such a system will not be optimal.

Business intelligence reports can still run on operational systems, but the process is slow. I have seen some reports require six hours to run, which is a poor timetable for decision-making. Similarly, very fast reporting can produce very slow transactions, prompting customers to avoid doing business to avoid long waits.

This long time required for generating or inserting of data will impact the system performance requirements, resulting in the system becoming slow from the customer or end user perspective. And then the blame game will start if it is an application problem or a database problem.

In other words, any system that slows down due to data load would equal a poorly designed system. You might need to build multiple systems that play well together to solve this issue.

The business analyst needs to be involved in this because of the nonfunctional performance and response time requirements. You need to highlight this to the SMEs during the application design to ensure the system can take a hit, especially if the system is planned to be used for years and generate millions of transactions. Any empty system will perform quickly, and a poorly designed system will cause the customer experience to degrade over time. So instead, work with the SMEs to build something that can handle the load, though it may take a sprint or two longer.

To create the right, valuable product for the end user, stay focused on the goal through each development segment, both in and out of production, to design the final solution. Accomplishing this will entail three distinct phases:

- Decide on the overall design
- Break it down into parts
- Plan how to assemble the parts

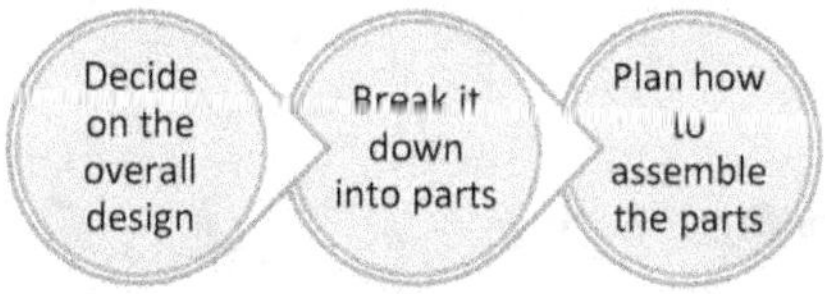

Figure 53 Design phases

In addition to the previous models mentioned earlier in the book, there are additional operational aspects that need consideration in order to be able to deliver as expected. Here are examples of common technologies used in the design process to overcome complexity and achieve agility.

Overall Design

The overall process and technology design can greatly help overcome most challenges. Ensuring that parts work tightly to overcome obstacles is key to smooth delivery. Misplacing the pieces can cause the entire process to fail or to fall short in delivering the required results. Please do not confuse this with the design of the application itself. This is the design of the process to ensure the smooth delivery and operation of the created system. Failure to adhere to this step can greatly increase the effort required to support, maintain, and even change or update your process to meet ever-shifting requirements. The majority of any application's life is spent in the operations phase, so it's worth the effort to ensure that you plan so that operations will be easier down the road. Here is an overview of just two technologies.

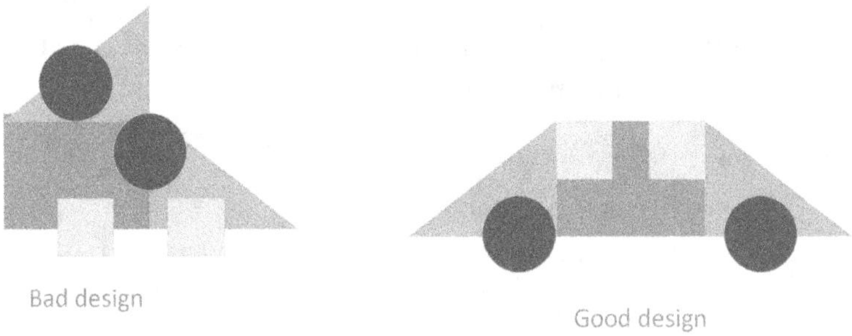

Figure 54 *Good versus bad design*

Site Reliability Engineering

The primary focus of site reliability engineering (SRE) is production support (the operations). The release manager controls the change to production. Deploying SRE calls for the smallest payload, as lean as possible, with options to roll back. Ideally, changes will rely on automation, not manual work. That means don't log into a server and make modifications. Instead, create a package with the change inside (this could be a script) and run the package on the system. It will be much easier to trace changes, generate a log, and, if needed, roll it back. It might seem as though clicking a button is easier than creating a script to accomplish the same function. But the goal is not to make this step easy. The idea is to make it traceable and repeatable for use in preproduction and production environments.

Always maintain a release website or other location to highlight changes. (A simple IIS server/Apache with a simple HTML page can accomplish this.) Then be sure to announce your change to everyone. Three concepts exist within SRE:

- **Self-service automation**: As the title implies, this is a do-it-yourself approach. Whatever is required to get the job done, you can do it yourself without relying on any process or having someone else deliver this piece of information to you (work in progress). This will significantly increase task accountability and help streamline the task's delivery.
- **Service level objectives**: These are the general goals and objectives of the service.
- **Error budget**: This is a budget dedicated to issues and errors. This might include the time allowed for a service to go down each year. If the budget runs out, changes to that service might be blocked during that period. The budget can be time or actual money.

Some Suggestions on How SRE Would Help

- The starting point is to build a release page to show what's going on on the development side.
- Have a discussion with the operations team and ask for the service level objectives to ensure the application can achieve the needed targets.
- Plan for error and release windows. The application might be able to release a valid version after every sprint, but this does not mean it will be released to production. Usually, there are testing and quality assurance phases after the development is completed. This is not a QA from the development team; it is the operational QA, such as stress tests, moving UAT, moving the application between environments (dev, test, QA, preproduction, production), and finally, the security scans. OPSQA usually takes a bit

more time, even if you have CI/CD, so always plan the releases.

- Provide the releases with complete documentation on how to deploy them and possible issues. This will provide some speed during the deployment phase.

Distributed Designs

Remember that every componant breaks, no matter what. Design systems that are resilient and capable of recovering quickly from errors. Reliability domains are the reason three 99 percent available components yield a lower availability rate (99 * 99 * 99 = 97). The underlying issue: the greater the number of components, the less reliable the system. Some apps use load balancers or store three copies of themselves so that a failure will not affect the system. The formula, in that case, will be (1 – (1 – .99)(1 – .99)(1 – .99) = .999999.

Testing for failures is important, so plan for failure and how you will recover. A failure detection system could be as simple as a script. A script generates a new server to pick up the load if the primary server fails. Still, the server will be deprovisioned if the load decreases to maintain the fewest possible parts to run the system and reduce the possibility of failure in this reliability domain. Always challenge reliability ideas by testing them. Don't depend on a cluster to function if one or more nodes fail. Test to ensure service continuity. The Chaos Monkey concept or similar system may play a major role in ensuring a system is resilient—and doesn't just look resilient—and that it will perform correctly in a failure.

Also, remember that the user expects the service and not the system. If the connection is down, they will report that the system is down and not that the link is down. When testing, test the whole service from the user's endpoint to the desired functionality.

The simplest way of doing this is to write down every part of the service on a piece of paper and pull a random one out of the stack. Whatever you pull out should go offline so you can see the effect. You should start with what-if scenarios and move gradually to logically disabling the component (unplug the network or shut it down).

Some Suggestions on How Distributed Designs Would Help

- There is no single point of failure; every component (except for the database) should have two active nodes and a load balancer in front of it. No single component should be able to stop the application.
- The database, due to many DBMS limitations, might not be able to have multiple active copies, but all DBMSs should have clustering functionality with one primary active server.
- Always test node failure and see how other components would react to that. Sometimes, if a node fails in a cluster, the cluster goes down entirely, and other times when a load-balanced node fails, the load balancer would still send some traffic to the failed node and not realize the failure occurred until the next health check.
- Include all of this in the documentation, and what cases the application should withstand. The customer might surprise you with specific failure cases.
- Always ask if the application would have a disaster recovery site.

Creating the Parts

This includes the component itself and what you need to fulfill the overall design. Determine how each block of the system will look and how it will meet the general needs of users. This becomes the system's building block and signals the need of each part. Usually, this is done through application modeling tactics. The smaller the parts, the better. These will be easier to replicate across different system parts and easier to move. This part will gain insights into two technologies, microservices and serverless computing.

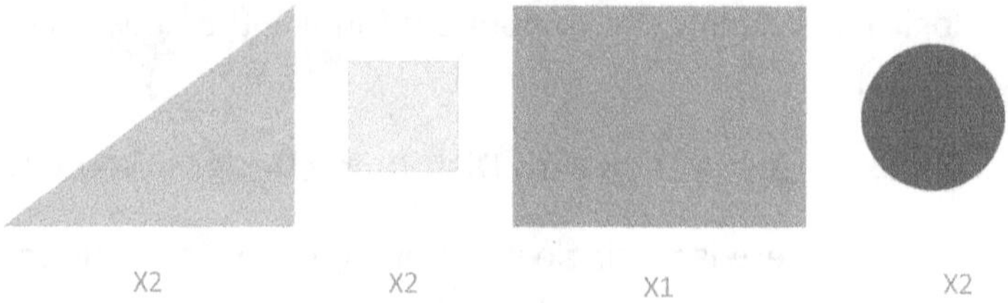

Figure 55 Required parts

Architecture

It helps to understand some options of application architecture.

1. **Monolithic architecture** is a single application package that performs several functions and deploys all at once. This is considered a single-tier, self-contained application and independent from other applications. It delivers complete function, not a single task. However, this dictates large-scale releases to patch or add features to the software.

2. **In service-oriented architecture (SOA)**, each application component is independent and uses communication protocol to communicate. Each part provides a specific service to other parts and produces a specified outcome, and each component is self-contained. The downside: it reports either an OK or an error but nothing in between. Typical software in SOA includes:

- A presentation layer
- A business process logic
- Data access

The problem in SOA relates to the connections. If the connections are too complicated, it will be easier to use a monolithic application.

3. **Microservices**: The idea behind microservices is to create the code or the system on a modular level. All communications are over API, and any unit can call any other unit in the system. The allure of it is its operation and elasticity. Each part is small, can be tested with a few scenarios, and can be deployed quickly. This allows the services to grow not for the maximum possible load but for the

average load. That provides for scalability whenever required because of its elasticity.

The primary problem with microservices is that if the software architect does not design a well-thought-out architecture design, things can get quite tricky after a while. Another issue with microservices is the number of artifacts that require maintenance. The more artifacts, the greater the complexity, and the less reliable the system would be. Microservices as a concept are quite good *if* executed correctly, so always validate the use case and why you need to build it this way. The business doesn't need it in many cases, and even a monolithic application will do the job well. But as mentioned, it's something new, and many people like to try new things. But a valid option to build a microservice is a scale system with millions of users who will use it daily—something like Amazon, Netflix, or a public service application. Otherwise, stick to SOA or monolithic.

Suppose someone is still insisting on the microservices concept. Then you could push it the other way, the IT operation way. It's the traditional three-tier architecture but over containers with orchestration and automation. Creating some microservices (as a concept) is possible, but the underlying programming will remain almost the same. So, think of this method as a modular monolithic. However, this is not technically a microservice but is widely accepted as one.

Serverless Computing

In a typical architecture, you have a client, HW, OS, app, server, and DB. Then virtualization abstract hardware. After that, the container abstracts OS, and the application in serverless abstracts the language runtime.

In serverless, each component performs a function and does not prominently exist on the system. You run it from the function, and then it's deleted. The application can chain several functions together. Each function triggers an event that creates another function until results are achieved. No central server governs the process. All functions are distributed. Serverless computing is an event-driven, compute-on-demand experience that implements codes triggered by events. When an event triggers it, it responds to that event. Then the code (function) is terminated. Serverless computing is cloud-based and is offered by three major vendors: Microsoft, AWS, and Google.

Benefits of Serverless

- Scaling is built in. The more conditions/events/requests generated, the more functions are created to serve these requests.
- Pay for the compute. Pay for what you need in 100MS compute time.
- There are no servers. As a concept, everything is fully automated as functions on the cloud.

The Cons of Serverless

- The operation model may be difficult to grasp.
- There is vendor lock-in.
- It does not replace server-oriented computing.
- There are limitations.
- It's not a fit for every need.
- Codes are run on a shared platform, which is a compliance issue under some standards.

When to Use

- New simple applications.
- Small applications or application use cases that serve a specific function.
- When a considerable value of scaling (need to scale fast but not for very long) is needed, like order processing on Black Friday.

Component Assembly

Proper application deployment is key to ensuring that results can be duplicated and that each part is well-known and correctly placed. Such a mechanism will allow parts to be generated from the templates as needed and scaled quickly in both directions, up and down. Containers are the clearest example of that.

Figure 56 Parts layout

Containers

Containers do not simplify the development life cycle. Instead, they increase the complexity of development by adding a layer (creating the container) to the mix. But they do make operation, maintenance, and support much easier. For example, the elements of the interface are more likely to change than the application logic. So, it's best to isolate them in a container and only change this part.

Also, many software vendors want to ensure the application functions correctly, so they create containers and hand them over to the customer to run on the OS. This is the same as the virtual appliance concept, but with containers.

Design Containers

Don't store data inside containers; the containers are short-lived. Typically, you'll use containers for microservices or the front end and middleware of the application but confine data to a database—either one monolithic database or multiple smaller databases.

It is possible to assemble as many instances as possible from a single container to process several parallel requests simultaneously. Rolling back and rolling forward will require an orchestration tool to automate deployment and container creation to simplify final service delivery. The same container can be moved between test and development, staging, preproduction, and production environments.

What Is Kubernetes?

Kubernetes is an open-source orchestration system for Docker containers. It handles scheduling nodes in a compute cluster and actively manages workloads to ensure their state matches design intentions.

Kubernetes is responsible for creating clusters and scaling up and down the containers as they run on a system that must quickly respond to changing business needs. Think Pokémon Go when it launched and had a massive surge before stabilizing. Scaling up and down will help meet the required demand for seasonal businesses.

Some vendors offer Kubernetes-branded options. Each has its vision. Seek one that simplifies the control, management, and automation processes if the business environment is demanding and has many change requests.

Chapter 7: Real-Life Deployment Consideration

In the previous chapter, you learned how to build the components, what technologies to use, and how to ensure the overall design is fit for use. In this chapter, the terms change between creating and deploying the code. You need to know how to plan the deployment of the last parts because they impact the operations significantly. It's possible to deploy one application on one server that delivers the same functions as an application on 10 servers. The difference will show when trying to scale the operations. So, it would help to consider the application architecture, where the code is running, and where the data is stored. Though this should have a minimal impact on the user requirements, it's considered good to know how things will fit to deliver the value needed by the end user.

Why Should You Be Concerned about the Operations Load?

The primary reason for that is that it impacts application performance and maintainability. It's a difficult balance to make it easy for the development team and make it quite challenging to operate and maintain or vice versa. The more it's built as separate components running on the cloud, the more time is invested in creating the application. On the other hand, that time will be recovered when updating or even fixing something.

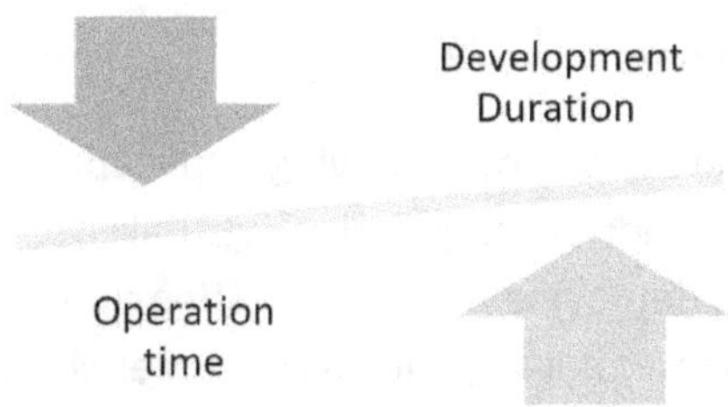

Figure 57 Development duration versus operations

How to Deploy the Application

Ideally, the application should be deployed in the cloud and/or using containers; deploying directly to servers is still a valid option, but it's not the best use of resources.

Deploy to Cloud

This part will determine the endpoints of the application that will be deployed to it. There are three cloud delivery models, though this is getting more complex by the day, and subcategories show up between the primary models almost every day. Always consider IaaS as entry-level only. Develop the application to run as SaaS or PaaS; it will be cheaper and have fewer operations issues.

IaaS (infrastructure as a service): A provider provides hardware, software, storage, and network.

SaaS (software as a service): A third-party entity provides hardware, software, storage, network, software provision, software maintenance, and updates. The end user provides operational data, only developing a few additional forms on the platform.

PaaS (platform as a service): A third-party entity provides hardware, software, storage, network, software maintenance, and updates. You provision the software on top of the platform and configure it (for example, container).

Selecting one of these elements will drive the decision on how the application could be made.

Deploy Using Containers

Containers are a way of deploying applications. Containers are not virtualization, nor do they replace virtualization. It's a modular approach to deploying and transporting applications. It works best with other technologies, such as microservices. Containers are growing year after year. They're expected to reach 100% of application delivery in seven to 10 years.

Why Containers?

- Agility
- Scalability/high availability
- Cost optimization
- Portability

Common Use Cases

- Continuous integration/continuous deployment (CI/CD) automation
- Autoscaling/microservice architecture
- Containers as a service
- Hybrid cloud architecture

Advantages

- Better resource utilization (same OS, multiple processes)
- Fewer application conflicts
- Can run the application on multiple OSs without getting a mismatched version (better application compatibility)
- Can copy the container between environments (production and preproduction)
- Easier release management

Plan the Required Resources (CPU, Memory, Storage, Network, Security)

Usually, this part falls outside of diagram and software development. But unfortunately, you need to plan it or at least understand the language required to deploy the application between the different components. You would need to secure the following with the operation teams as well:

- CPU
- Memory
- Storage

It would help if you considered three things (or at least ensure they are OK with the network and security teams):

- Bandwidth requirements

- Security requirements (protocols, ports, and encryption)
- Authentication

Plan Storage Requirements

Currently, the GB cost is very cheap. Even TB is not that expensive anymore. It's rare to run into issues related to storage size. But suppose the application has thousands of connections per second. In that case, it's strongly recommended that storage performance be solid-state or all-flash to ensure the right input/output operations per second (IOPS). Still, generally, the storage requirements combine many different things. You should consider the size of the:

- Application files
- Runtime files (server files)
- Logic engine–required space (like the web server, for example)
- Database engine
- Reporting engine size
- Data storage size (usually, it follows a calculation similar to the network, but you use the insert size per user)
- Temp generated files
- Log files

This excludes the OS requirements, of course.

The final requirement is the IOPS requirements, or how many simultaneous operations are needed per second. This is based on how many transactions need to be generated. A simple laptop HDD (*not* SSD) can handle up to 200 operations per second. You will have at least three disks in a server; if it's on the low end, it can generate enough power to have 25 to 50 users browsing the application simultaneously.

Plan the Memory Requirements

Usually, memory requirements comprise two main parts:

- *Working memory* is where the application is uploaded to execute. It should contain the engines of the database and the application server, part of the runtime, and all the application files + in-progress files + the user's active sessions

- *Cache memory* is used to speed up performance. This is the entirety of the database + active transactions not yet committed to the log file and files needed by the engine to render the website and the application.

Plan the CPU Requirements

Nowadays, processors are pretty efficient, so you will not run into any problems unless the application runs on old hardware, but typically, two processors will suffice for a typical workload. If you are running on a cloud, start with the minimum possible cycles, and if the processing peaks at 100% most of the time, then move up one step. But if you need to perform the calculation for some reason, page load testers can simulate a connection. You can use a tool like Selenium to simulate a load. Use Jmeter to stress-test the server. This will give an average of the expected load per user profile.

Plan the Network Communications and Bandwidth Requirements

The starting point is the deployment diagram.

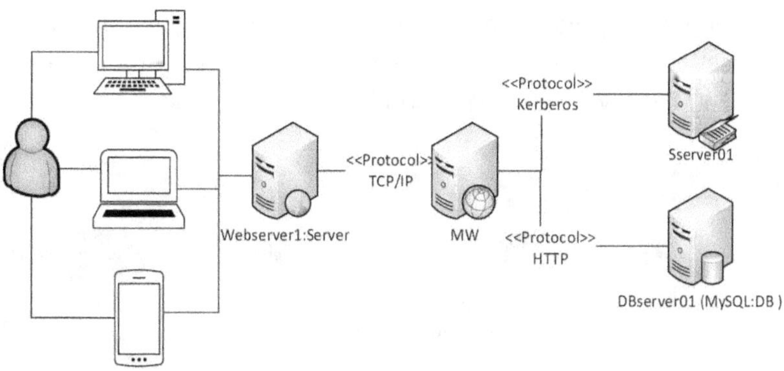

- **Network bandwidth** is the maximum bit rate per second measured in bits (100MB,1G,10G). Divide by 8 to get the byte value, resulting in a 1G connection that can transfer only 128 MB per second. This is very slow for a server. Virtualization will reach a maximum of 80% of the physical network; the remaining 20% will be consumed in the translation/network layer.

- **Latency** is the round-trip duration of the packet.

The above two items are critical to calculating the app's network bandwidth and the time-out duration. And for the network bandwidth, find out how many calls could be sent per connection. It's a formula that includes:

- Expected users count (N).
- Expected number of requests (R)
- The average size per request (S)
- The expected number of connections (C)

From the online bookstore example, let's assume the application has 25 expected users. Each user opens the website and browses five books on average. The average request size is calculated based on the sequences of calls you generate. So, to simplify, let's assume each call is an average of 200KB, except for the last call, which is 3MB. (5 * 200 + 1 * 3072)/6 = 670KB (per call).

Note: The expected number of users and how many users would browse this information should be determined from the business side. If they did not research this, ask them to guess at a number to set the expectation. If the application expects 20 users but gets 2000, this would be a big problem.

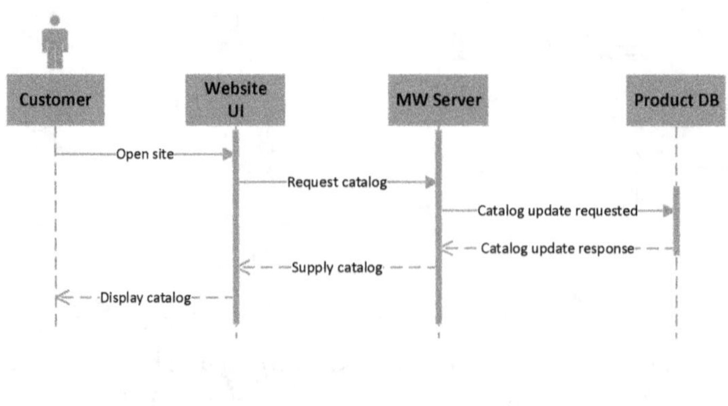

Figure 58 Part of the sequence diagram

Now let's calculate how many jumps this call will go through (the network parts of the deployment diagram show four connections. For each average user, 670KB jumping four connections = 2700KB (2.7MB) per user).

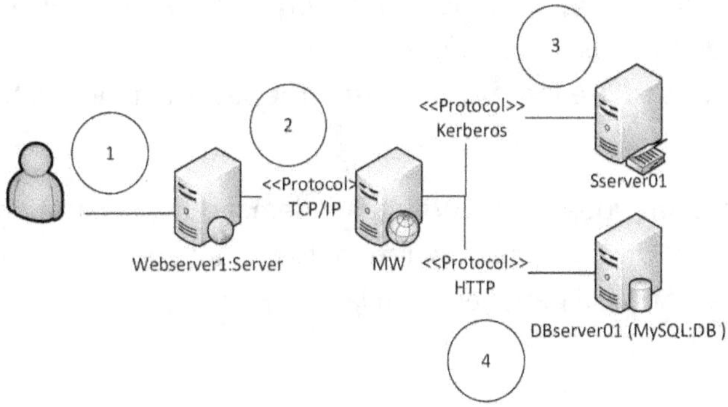

Figure 59 Connections gates

The total number of users is 25 * 2.7 = 67MB required. This calculation is the "per second calculation." Twenty-five users per second is a big number for a small shop. (This means they should get 90,000 customers per hour; usually, it's more like 0.002 customers per hour or less.)

These calculations are indicative of the requirements. The actual requirements will appear after monitoring the production environment for some time. The reason for doing this is to shorten the gap between planned users and reality.

Plan Security Requirements

Now let's look at the security components.

Protocols: Define the protocols used; some protocols are disallowed in the network, and the intrusion prevention system might block some application calls. So, ensure that both the system call and the protocols are allowed.

Ports: The ports used on the server are both source and destination to ensure the firewall will not block the connection.

Encryption: It might seem a good idea to encrypt everything from the application itself. But actually, the security team will help generate the security key, and they might require some connections to be unencrypted to detect any attack on the system.

Authentication: Will the application hold the security information inside it, or use a specific authentication repository to allow other services to use it as well? Consult the security team on how to do that.

Location: Does the security team demand the separation of each application layer in a separate network, and does the traffic need to pass a firewall between each layer?

Final Notes

At this point, you now have a solid document that should help address the major concerns when building an application by following this book. This is sometimes called a *high-level design*, or HLD. As mentioned at the beginning of the book, it's not the business analyst's responsibility to design the application. Still, if they failed to capture that this application would be required to serve 1 million users per day, this would change the picture for the development team. Being a product manager or BA demands more technical discussions. This was a primary objective to enable you to discuss these with the SMEs and ask them to perform these functions to confirm the overall application understanding. Ensure that the business requests what the team delivers while maintaining enough agility to change based on the new requirements.

www.ingramcontent.com/pod-product-compliance
Lightning Source LLC
LaVergne TN
LVHW022055200926
848481LV00003B/916